BOSSED UP

100 TRUTHS TO BECOMING YOUR OWN BOSS, GOD'S WAY!

CONT

ENTS

Tamar Huggins Publishing Inc. Toronto, Ontario, Canada.

WWW.TAMARHUGGINS.COM

Library and Archives Canada Cataloguing in Publication

Huggins, Tamar, Author

Bossed Up: 100 Truths to Becoming Your Own Boss, God's Way!

ISBN 978-0-9952120-0-8 (Paperback)

ISBN 978-0-9952120-1-5 (E-book)

COVER DESIGN	Nicholas Bacquie, www.nikodidit.com
PHOTOGRAPHY	Jalani Morgan, www.jalanimorgan.com
BOOK DESIGN	Cecilia Perriard
EDITOR	Lenita Davis, Right Words Editing
PROOFREADER	Ameesha Green
MAKEUP	Andre C. Glashen
HAIR	Shan Morgan, Hair Enhanced Beauty Bar
HAIR	Khary Benjamin, Blade Runner Barber Shop
SET DESIGN	Sherryl Cole-Griffiths, Inside 7
LOCATION	Wendy Tumba, House of Tumba

PRINTED AND BOUND IN CANADA

DEDICATION

This book is dedicated to my Auntie,
Mrs. Inez Aneita Roach.
Thank you for the insurmountable love
you gave to me as a child.
I am who I am today because of it.
R.I.P.

ABOUT THE AUTHOR

Tamar is an award-winning serial entrepreneur, who has been featured exclusively in media outlets around the world including: *Black Entertainment Television*, *Canadian Living*, and *The Huffington Post*.

In 2012, Tamar founded *DRIVEN Accelerator Group*, a nonprofit organization committed to improving the socio-economic status of marginalized people through technology-based programming. She developed DRIVEN Startups—an advanced training program for tech entrepreneurs. Tamar also founded *Tech Spark*, a technology and design school for inner city youth.

Prior to *DRIVEN*, Tamar launched *Knexxion Communication Group*, a boutique PR agency with a focus on media, entertainment, and sports clientele. She spent the early years of her career as a Digital Media Planner for *H&M*, *Nike Canada*, and *Cadbury Adams*.

In 2015, Tamar was named the *Harry Jerome Young Entrepreneur*, and honored as one of *100 Black Women to Watch*. In 2016, Tamar launched *The CEO Project*, an online training company that teaches business success using Godly principles.

Tamar holds an advanced diploma from Centennial College in Creative Advertising, and Humber College in Public Relations. Tamar is very active in her Christian community, a wife, and mother of one.

ACKNOWLEDGEMENTS

This book would have never come to fruition if it wasn't for God placing this baby inside of me. I am so honored and humbled to be used by You in such a way as this.

Rory Grant: Thank you for believing in me, cheering me on, and encouraging me when I felt like giving up. You being proud of me means everything.

Talia-Mari Grant: A good woman leaves an inheritance to her children's children. Everything I do is for you.

Charles and Mavis Huggins: Thank you for doing your best for me. I am where I am today because of your determination to see me succeed.

Wendy Tumba and Sherryl Cole-Griffiths: Thanks for being my two amazingly talented and gifted big sisters! I looked up to you both as a child, and I still do. I want to thank you both for supporting me and encouraging me. I thank God for placing you both in my life. Your presence has helped shaped me into the successful businesswoman I am today.

Vanessa Wheatle: Thank you for being my friend, spiritual mother, and pastor. Thank you for your obedience to God's Word and for prophesying the existence of this book to me. You believed in me from the beginning, and you continue to encourage and push me to be all that God has called me to be. Thank you.

TO PURCHASE ADDITIONAL ITEMS MENTIONED IN THIS BOOK SUCH AS THE *BOSS JOURNAL* VISIT WWW.TAMARHUGGINS.COM

Introduction

I wasn't a college dropout. I wasn't a teen mom. I didn't grow up poor or come from the 'hood'. My story isn't the common "rags to riches" tale you hear from most people. The trials and circumstances of my journey birthed a greatness in me. Along with it came wisdom and experiences that are bound to prosper others.

I grew up in Brampton, a suburb of Toronto. I lived in a nice, middle-class neighborhood with both working parents, an older sister, and an aunt who was like my second mother. In seventh grade, I was introduced to the idea of business as a career option. Although I didn't fully understand what it was, I was fascinated with the idea of business.

As an adult, I experienced what it was like to be broke, bullied by seemingly soulless leaders, and discouraged by the ones I love. However, I soon learned that great suffering produces great character. ***Focus*** gave me the determination necessary to push through tough challenges because I kept the ultimate goal in mind. ***Confidence*** helped me to set high expectations (and meet them!) because I knew who I was in Christ. It was my ***wild ambition*** that earned the titles: "Canadian Superhero," "Entrepreneur of the Year," and "Top Black Woman to Watch." I didn't require anyone else's validation. God validated me, and I validated myself.

When the recession hit in 2009, I lost my job. My main client at the time fired the ad agency I worked for, and there was no work left for me to do. I had endured so much bullying in the workplace that it caused me emotional and physical distress in addition to the failing economy. Eventually, the ad agency started making cutbacks, and I was a part of that process. I believe the layoff was God's way of saying, "Enough is enough. I have so much more for you!" As a result, I went back to school and started a PR agency to explore my passions and to pay the bills.

In 2010, a few months after the birth of my daughter, the Lord revealed His will for my life through a prophetic word. He used my close friend to tell me that He was preparing to take me to heights I could never imagine. The Lord said I was going to be an author and a school principal. He also said that I was going to help people bring their business ideas to life. ***Umm...No!*** I thought. The other things I could live with, but I wasn't about to go back to school to become a teacher and then a principal. It just wasn't happening. (***You'll never believe how this turned out...we'll come back to this later in the book.***)

The next three years were professionally rewarding, yet very rough for me personally. I created my nonprofit – DRIVEN Accelerator Group – in January 2012. This company quickly gained international press coverage and several accolades. My team and I provided educational resources and training to brand new tech startups and helped our first cohort raise $1.1 million in startup capital. While the success of the company looked amazing, I found myself swimming in $20,000 worth of debt behind closed doors. In October of the same year, I lost my aunt to cancer. She was a mother to me, and I had never been so devastated in all my life. Two days before she passed, she called me to her bedside, peered into my eyes, and said what would be her last words to me: "You are the winner. You are the winner. You ARE the winner!" I had no idea what it meant at the time, but through the years, it became a reminder of the victorious power God had placed over my life.

She was right, as the year of 2015 was a groundbreaking year for me. I became debt-free and got married. My nonprofit raised over a quarter million dollars to launch my dream technology and design school for inner-city youth – Tech Spark. I was awarded as the Harry Jerome Entrepreneur of the Year and honored as one of 100 Black Women to Watch. Then in 2016 I was declared a "Canadian Superhero" by *Canadian Living Magazine* for my entrepreneurial pursuits within the community.

"To whom much is given, much will be required." (Luke 12:48) God isn't finished with me yet. I am His vessel, and He has called me to help you along the path to becoming your own boss. Whether it's overcoming the fear of rejection or understanding your true purpose, I'm game. You will find that this book is full of the valuable information and insights that guided – ***and still guide*** – my path to success. ***Bossed Up*** is meant to be read with a study Bible and your ***Boss Journal***, as you will be required to dig deeper into yourself and the Word of God. There are 100 ***Boss Truths*** plus 10 ***Boss Challenges***, and these will provoke new perspectives as you move into action. It is my prayer that these Truths, Challenges, and Tips prosper and enrich your life as you journey down the road of entrepreneurship.

Let's Get Bossed Up!

CHAPTER 1

GOD

BOSS TRUTH #1

MAKE GOD THE CEO OF YOUR BUSINESS

"Unless the Lord builds the house, they labor in vain who build it."
–PSALM 127:1

What does it mean to make God your CEO? Well, it's simple. Every business needs a leader, a visionary, one that can steer the ship and chart the course. That's a CEO, your Chief Executive Officer, the big boss, the one everybody reveres because they produce consistent results. For me, my CEO is and forever will be my Heavenly Father, and I am totally unapologetic about it. One of the great things about putting God in charge of all of my businesses is that He is very clear on the direction I need to take and steps I need to follow to be successful. He provides me with strategic direction, wisdom, and insight. It can't get any better than that, trust me.

How do I get this direction? God speaks to me through prophetic words and dreams. For example, the Lord used a close friend of mine to speak into my life in 2010. He told me three specific things I would do:

1. Write a book. (***Done – you're reading it!)***
2. Become a principal of a school. (***Done – more on that later!***)
3. Help bring the business ideas of others to LIFE. (***Done and still doing it!***)

I was excited about #1 and #3, but I said, "No! Absolutely not!" to #2. I was not about to go back to school to become a teacher and then a principal. Nope. I wasn't doing it. After having my daughter and running a PR agency at the same time, I was done with the idea of school. Little did I know, God had already planted the seed in me with this prophetic word – an idea that was to come forth.

Good businesses are birthed out of the pain an individual feels for which there is no solution. It pained my heart to see young people moving in a downward spiral, going back and forth like the pendulum in a grandfather clock. Some had no aim or direction, and seeing parents and teachers give up on them pained me even more. Since my Bishop taught me that my pains were an indication of my true passion, I began to explore it.

In 2015, my exploration led me to launch Tech Spark — a nonprofit technology and design school. It took three long years to finally receive funding to launch my dream project, as funders thought my idea was ahead of its time (not to mention, obtaining grants in Toronto is highly competitive).

At Tech Spark, our mission is clear: "Teach inner-city kids how to create the technology they use every day and to explore career and entrepreneurial opportunities with the skills gained in class." Now, while I don't teach any of the classes, I hire the people who do. I focus on the operations of the school, support staff in upholding our mission, and document the challenges and successes of our students. In essence, I ***am*** the principal of Tech Spark. When God spoke to me, I misinterpreted His message. My thinking was so linear at the time that I didn't see His vision clearly. Consequently, I subconsciously put limits on myself!

God wants us to seek Him before we try to figure it all out. Now that I think about it, this was probably His way of adding a sweet element of surprise once I realized exactly what He wanted me to do. Making God your CEO is all about knowing Him, trusting Him, and making what He says a priority. I know Him through dreams and prophecy, but your experience might be different. To know when He's speaking to you, you must know what His Word says and what His communication style is like with you. He might speak to you during your prayer and study time or through a message from a friend. No matter how you hear from Him, your challenge is to start listening! Write down how God communicates with you, and then begin to anticipate His voice.

NOTES

BOSS TRUTH #2

BE OBEDIENT TO THE WILL OF GOD

"If you are willing and obedient, you shall eat the good of the land."
–ISAIAH 1:19

Do you remember hearing your parent tell you to do something as a child simply because he or she said so? Wasn't that irritating? I bet it caused you to show some defiance and rebellion, right? As we reach maturity and become adults, many of us begin to realize our parents were right all along. Most of the trouble we got ourselves into could have been avoided if we had just listened. Our relationship with our Heavenly Father is much like our relationships with our mother and father figures. When God instructs us to do something that we don't want to do, we often rebel and suffer unnecessary consequences.

This form of disobedience can only lead to unfruitfulness and destruction. God has called us all to accomplish very specific goals, and He created us with the personalities, skills, and talents to achieve the goals He has set for our lives. When we think we have it all figured out and go down a path that wasn't intended for us, we fail. This can cause us to encounter a lot of hardships, and no matter what we do, nothing seems to work. Consequently, we become unhappy and blame those around us, including God. Your childhood self wouldn't dare tell your parents what to do (if you were raised like I was). It just doesn't work that way. As an adult, you should give God that same respect.

So what do you do when what God wants isn't what you want? Pray for an obedient heart! Remember I told you about my prophetic word from God? Well, I didn't want to become the principal of a school. The idea didn't thrill me at all. However, I knew if God was calling me to do it, I couldn't run from it. I asked the Lord to show me exactly what He meant for me. The more I prayed about the new direction, researched the industry, and received confirmation, I knew I was on the right path, and I became excited about it.

I challenge you to ask the Lord to strip away any form of disobedience from your heart. Pray and ask God to reveal His will for your life in a clear way that you can understand. For those areas you don't understand, pray that He increases your faith so you can walk boldly in His will. Pray for and be willing to allow the Holy Spirit to guide you in all areas so that you do not slip or stumble, but instead reap the rewards God has for you.

NOTES

BOSS TRUTH #3

PRIORITIZE PRAYER

"Now this is the confidence that we have in Him, that if we ask anything according to His will, He hears us. And if we know that He hears us, whatever we ask, we know that we have the petitions that we have asked of Him."

–1 JOHN 5:14-15

I can't even begin to tell you how important it is to pray and fast for the things we desire. I'm not talking about praying once a day, but several times a day. Prayer is so simple, but we complicate it. We often think that we don't have eloquent words to express our hearts' desires, or we simply don't make time for it. Prayer is so much more than hurriedly reciting, "Our Father, which art in heaven..." before we fall asleep. It is a deep, personal, and intimate time that we share alone with God. You may think He doesn't hear you, but trust me, He knows your heart's desires before you even know them.

The scripture Psalm 37:4 tells us, "Delight yourself also in the Lord, and He shall give you the desires of your heart." This doesn't mean pray once and forget about the request you've made. It means seek to do what is pleasing to the Lord and whatever gives glory to His Kingdom, and He will give you what you ask for if it's His will. What can you do every day to please the Lord? Show interest! Ladies, there is nothing more frustrating than a guy who shows interest in you, disappears for weeks at a time, then pops up out of nowhere and acts like nothing happened. We, women, love attention, and so does God. Show interest in the things of the Lord! Study your Bible, download a daily devotional app, treat people the way He treats you, and be consistent! It's really as simple as that.

Fasting is a powerful addition to prayer. When we add fasting to our prayer life, breakthroughs happen. Adding fasting to prayer is like adding rocket boosters to a shuttle. Even though the shuttle can fly on its own, the rocket boosters make for a more effective liftoff and powerful propulsion into a targeted area. Fasting makes our prayers more fiery, focused, and dangerous to the enemy! When we fast, we deny ourselves of food, the phone, or social media for a specific amount of time. When we rid ourselves and our environments of distractions, our spirit can more freely connect with His. You're basically saying, "Lord, here I am!" He is then able to download all that you need into your spirit, and you generally come out of the fast feeling refreshed, charged up, and ready to take action!

Making prayer a priority is a process that requires stillness. Stillness can be difficult to achieve when you have a million other things going on in your life. So you must carve out a special time when you can pray openly and honestly about the desires of your heart, read the Word of God, and meditate. Find your "prayer closet" wherever it may be, lock yourself away, and just talk to your Father. He wants to hear from you, and He wants to bless you. Just ask.

BOSS TIP

Have you ever felt like you don't know *how* to pray?
Try the *R.A.T.P.* method.

***Repentance:* Before you do anything, you must confess and ask forgiveness for all sins, both known and unknown.**

***Adoration:* Spend time here telling God how much you love him. Make him feel nice!**

***Thanksgiving:* Thank God for all He has done, and all He is about to do.**

***Petition:* This is where you make your request, and ask God for your heart's desires.**

NOTES

BOSS TRUTH #4

NO ONE EVER CONQUERED THE WORLD WHILE STANDING STILL

"Thus also faith by itself, if it does not have works, is dead. But someone will say, 'You have faith, and I have works.' Show me your faith without your works, and I will show you my faith by my works."
– JAMES 2:17-18

Some people ask for things, and sit with their hands open waiting for a blessing to come to them. Do you know people like this? If so, how has the sitting and waiting worked out for them? The most actionable thing to do is ***get up and move***. If you want to start a business, pray for profitable ideas, but don't sit and wait for success to come to you. You have to go after it! Get on your computer, research your industry, go to events, and meet new people. Once you've made up in your mind that this opportunity is what you want, you need to position yourself to receive the blessing. Ask yourself, "What do I need to do right now before this blessing arrives? How can I prepare myself to handle all that I've asked God for?"

One of my favourite stories is found in 2 Kings 3. God sent an army of Israelites to conquer Moab, and for seven days they marched to the land and became tired and very thirsty. King Jehoshaphat went to the Prophet Elisha to ask for guidance. In verses 17-18, Elisha tells King Jehoshaphat, "Thus says the Lord: 'Make this valley full of ditches.' For thus says the Lord: 'You shall not see wind, nor shall you see rain; yet that valley shall be filled with water, so that you, your cattle, and your animals may drink. And this is a simple matter in the sight of the Lord; He will also deliver the Moabites into your hand.' " It sounds crazy, right? Who wants to dig ditches in the desert when they are already tired and thirsty?! ***And*** when was the last time anyone saw water in the desert? With God, all things are possible. Providing your blessing is but a light thing for the Lord to do, ***but you must prepare yourself to receive the blessing or you will risk missing it***.

I challenge you to move from a place of asking to a place of preparation and expectation. If you're unsure about what steps to take, pray about it and ask the Holy Spirit to guide you. Remember to be open to the various ways this blessing can come to you. Sometimes, all it takes is being in the right place at the right time to hear a word that triggers your blessing. If the Lord answered your prayer tomorrow, would you be ready to receive it? If not, address what's stopping you. Make a list of obstacles that are preventing you from achieving your goal. Begin to push past whatever is holding you back by asking the Lord to direct your steps. ***Put your faith to work.***

NOTES

BOSS TRUTH #5

IT TAKES BOTH THE SUN AND THE RAIN TO GROW

*"We also glory in tribulations,
knowing that tribulation produces
perseverance; and perseverance,
[produces] character;
and character, hope."*
–ROMANS 5:3-4

The Greek word for ***suffer***[1] means to "hold one's self upright; endure, bear patiently," and the Greek word for ***character***[2] means "approval through testing."[1] Each one of us has a story to tell. That story is our testimony. A testimony is brought about by trying circumstances, and when we look back at them, we see how far we've come and how much we've grown. What is your story? What is it about the challenges you've faced that makes you who you are today? Our testimonies are directly linked to our purpose. Testimonies are stories of triumph that we share through our words. They are our connecting point into the hearts of others.

Consider the story of Naomi and Ruth. Naomi was moved to dwell in a foreign land because of famine in her own country. While there, she bore more grief at the death of her husband, and then of her two sons. So as widows with no resources, she and her daughter-in-law Ruth traveled back to Naomi's home of Bethlehem in hope of God's provision. Ruth, who was not a native of Bethlehem, could have chosen to remain in her own home with her own family during this time of sorrow. Instead, she stayed with Naomi. Her faithfulness and strength yielded great favor in the sight of Boaz. With the help of Naomi's wisdom, she went from gleaning in his fields to eating among the reapers to acquiring redemption for the land of her deceased husband as well as Naomi's husband. In the end, Boaz takes Ruth as his wife and God causes her to conceive a son and become part of the lineage of Christ. Their testimony is one of great triumph because of their steadfastness, faith, and unity. We mustn't be ashamed of our story, because it makes us who we are.

BOSS TRUTH #6

ALLOW GOD TO BUILD YOUR TEAM

"So the Lord said to Moses: Gather to Me seventy men of the elders of Israel, whom you know to be the elders of the people and officers over them..." "Then the Lord came down in the cloud, and spoke to him, and took of the Spirit that was upon him, and placed the same [Spirit] upon the seventy elders…"
–NUMBERS 11:16A, 25A

Every boss needs a team, a "ride or die" crew, that will help take their vision to the next level. You may be ready to build your team, but you don't know exactly who you need. This is where the gift of discernment comes into play. Discernment literally means that you are able to see and/or know which spirits are of God and which aren't. We all have a spirit within us: some people have good spirits, and others have evil spirits. When you have a strong business idea, you may find that everyone wants to jump on the bandwagon just to say, "Yeah, I'm a part of that," or "I helped start that company." So you need to be very careful of who you allow to join your team. It's sad to say, but some people only want to see what you're doing so they can copy or destroy you.

In the beginning stages of building my business, I spent the first months working alone. When I realized I needed a board to run my business more effectively, I searched **LinkedIn** based on the skills I knew I needed. I used discernment to narrow down who I approached for a spot on my team. It may sound funny to you, but I was able to look at someone's photo and see their spirit. If my spirit didn't get a good vibe from their photo, I didn't even bother to connect with them. The individuals I chose to reach out to gave me an immediate yes, because the vision was strong and my nonprofit had the potential to create major impact. Four years later, we are still going strong. We became more than associates; we became close friends. I truly believe that my team is made up of angels because let me tell you, if it wasn't for them, I wouldn't be where I am today. So many doors of opportunities and countless blessings came my way, all because of who was a part of my team.

An important step in building your team is to research common business models for your industry in order to understand what skills, personality types, and levels of experience are needed. After that, I want you to identify your own skills and talents, and create a list of everything that is missing. Pray for the Lord to give you the gift of discernment of spirits. Ask

Him to send you individuals with the key skills you've identified, plus anything else you may have missed. Be attentive over the next several weeks and months. Don't just sit and wait for people to come to you. Put yourself in a position where you can meet new people. When you feel you've found someone, test the spirit. The Holy Spirit will let you know whether that person is God-sent, or whether they are a decoy.

NOTES

BOSS TRUTH #7

IF YOU SOW THE SEED, YOU WILL REAP THE REWARDS

"He who sows sparingly will also reap sparingly, and he who sows bountifully will also reap bountifully. So let each one give as he purposes in his heart, not grudgingly or of necessity; for God loves a cheerful giver. And God is able to make all grace abound toward you, that you, always having all sufficiency in all things, may have an abundance for every good work."
–2 CORINTHIANS 9:6-8

I cannot express how important it is to tithe. Tithing is simply giving 10% of your earnings back to the Kingdom of God. I say "back to" because your wealth comes from God. I understand that many people don't give, or when they do, they aren't happy about it. They dread the collection plate and think of all the things they'd rather do with their tithe. I get it. I wasn't always a cheerful giver myself. As entrepreneurs, our financial stability is dependent on how quickly we make a sale, or receive compensation for our work. Sometimes, the money doesn't come in when we need it to – and when it finally does, the last thing we tend to think about is donations. Am I right, or am I right?

The scripture tells us that we should give with a cheerful heart. Why? When we give, the Lord blesses us in many ways. Now I'm not saying you should give only because you want something back. When we don't invest back into the Kingdom of God, we tie up the blessings He has for us. For example, your business may begin to move slowly, people will begin to owe you money, major repairs for your car spring out of nowhere, etc. It's all a consequence of robbing God of what's rightfully His. When we do give, God provides us with bountiful opportunities, such as the obvious – more money! As children of God, we are to pray, sow, call the rain, and reap the harvest. You should give as a way of telling God, "Thanks." Imagine it like this: you have a business partner, and all they require is 10% of the profit for everything they do – not 50% or 80% ***but 10%*** – and you get to keep 90%! Sounds like a pretty sweet deal to me.

BOSS TRUTH #8

YOU ARE NOT SELF-MADE

"I am the vine; you are the branches.
He who abides in Me, and I in him,
bears much fruit; for without
Me you can do nothing."
–JOHN 15:5

"Self-made" is a trendy term that people use to prove how much of a "boss" they are. ***Please don't follow the hype.*** I can never understand how anyone can honestly say they are self-made. It just doesn't make sense to me; no one can truly become successful on their own. Every business needs customers, leaders, mentors, etc. Somewhere along the way, someone or something helped you on the path to success. For me, it was all the people God blessed me with throughout my life. He strategically placed family members, friends, even strangers in my life to provide support in the areas I needed it the most. God was there every step of the way – from ideation to building my team and launching my businesses. I wish I could claim all the wonderful things I've done as my own original ideas, but the truth is that I allowed God to download every single idea into my spirit. Accordingly, over the course of seven years, I've seen many of those ideas grow into solid brands and impactful movements. There is no shame in admitting that you need help. In fact, no one – and I mean no one – can do it alone. Don't aspire to be a self-made entrepreneur, but rather a God-made entrepreneur. Allow the Lord to build you the way He intended you to be.

BOSS TRUTH #9

BE THANKFUL

—

"In everything give thanks; for this is the will of God in Christ Jesus for you."
–1 THESSALONIANS 5:18

Feeling gratefulness and thanksgiving in your heart is one of the best things you can do for your spiritual and physical self. You may not always feel like you have it all together, but I know you have things in your life that you can feel grateful for, even at this very moment. For instance, I'm grateful that my husband understands when I really need to focus on my work. He makes sure that our daughter's homework is complete and that she's taken care of and entertained while I work painstakingly to meet deadlines. I thank God for that because, alternatively, he could be like some men who believe taking care of the children is a woman's job. Even though my husband and I believe that women and men should share the parenting responsibilities equally, I show appreciation to my husband by simply saying, "Thank you," or "I noticed what you did for me."

If we as businesswomen and men overlook the kindness that someone has shown toward us, how then can we feel worthy of kindness from others? Take a moment to ask yourself, "Has someone done something for me that I haven't acknowledged yet?" If so, thank that person. A simple handwritten note can really show a tremendous amount of appreciation. I challenge you to thank the Lord each morning for ten things that you are grateful for. It could be something small like a noticeable increase in your Instagram followers or something great like waking up with a sound mind. The key is to always remain thankful and to show appreciation even for the smallest of things.

BOSS TRUTH #10

YOUR BUSINESS IS NOT YOUR GOD

*"You shall have
no other gods before Me."*
–EXODUS 20:3

As a boss, you will work very hard to turn your dreams into reality. Sometimes, you'll do it with little help from anyone around you, and you'll feel like it's just you alone. I've felt that way many times. I would put all my efforts toward ensuring my success to the point that I neglected other areas of my life. ***I was obsessed with it***. My business had become my god, and because I knew I was doing the will of God, I thought it was acceptable. I was so carried away with work most of the time that I missed birthday parties, cherished moments with family, and opportunities to meet new friends. Before I could move forward, God had to show me the error in my approach. He had to take some things away from me before I could realize the importance of placing Him first and showing appreciation for the important things in my life. We have to be mindful of how we divide our attention into the various areas of our lives. A simple formula for success is: God ***first***, Family ***second***, and Work ***third***. God has so much in store for you, but you have to chase Him more than anything or anyone else.

BOSS CHALLENGE #1

I simply challenge you to draw nearer to God. Throughout this chapter, I've given you ways to make God a part of your business and everyday life. Now, I challenge you to actually do it. Make God the CEO of your life and business. If you don't have a home church, ask God to direct you to one that will help nurture you. If you don't know where to begin reading in your Bible, start with a daily devotional and read the corresponding scriptures. The power to grow is in your hands.

NOTES

CHAPTER 2

FASCINATE

BOSS TRUTH #11

BE 100% YOU

"Then God said, Let us make man in Our image, according to Our likeness... So God created man in His own image, in the image of God He created him; male and female He created them."

–GENESIS 1:26A, 27

Of the seven billion people and counting on this earth, God created you unlike anyone else. You have your own unique fingerprint, personality traits, and talents. To be successful, you don't have to change who you are, but rather become ***more*** of who you are. A few years ago, I remember feeling and thinking that I was boring. I am an introvert, and prefer to work behind the scenes. I wore my career achievements on my sleeve, because I was proud of them. My career was the only topic I was comfortable discussing. I felt like my life only consisted of work. ***"I'm not fun; I need to get a life,"*** I said. Then a good friend of mine told me, "You're not boring, Tamar, you just have to allow people to get to know you." At that moment, I realized that I didn't have to be outgoing or the life of the party for people to notice the person behind the brands I created.

People were naturally attracted to my confidence, wit, and ambition. My ability to set high expectations and meet them was how I inspired people the most. I didn't have to be the loudest, prettiest, or smartest person. I just had to be more of myself. I want you to aspire to be the best possible version of yourself. Find ways to understand why others are fascinated by you. How does the world see you? What makes you special? Is it your ability to show people how great they can become? Perhaps it's your knack of coming up with fresh solutions to stale problems. Whatever it may be, own it! ***Don't aspire to be anyone else.*** Authenticity outshines perfection. Being 100% you beats trying to be 100% perfect, every day.

BOSS TRUTH #12

REJECT MEDIOCRITY

"The soul of a lazy man desires, and has nothing; But the soul of the diligent shall be made rich."
–PROVERBS 13:4

T. D. Jakes once said, "Some people want the product but don't want to go through the process." Just like a diamond in the rough, success comes out of exceptional pressure and diligent work. We are all ***created in the image of God***, so to be mediocre is simply not of God! Are you ready and willing to go outside your comfort zone to achieve greatness? You can be comfortable or you can be outstanding, but you can't be both.

Think of Peter and how uncomfortable his experiences were while walking so closely with Jesus. He was often openly rebuked and even once called Satan.[3] ***Ouch.*** His character was challenged, his misguided zeal was restrained,[4] and once he was even silenced by God Himself.[5] But in his passion and great determination, he never gave up. In his uncomfortableness, his destiny was being shaped and molded, and he was being made ready[6] for something the world had never seen. If you fast-forward to the book of Acts, you see God's power on display in Peter in such a grand way as he led one of the greatest movements of the early church.[7] The things Peter endured and the lessons he learned caused God to extend His trust toward Peter. And it means that his season of discomfort wasn't meant to break him, but to build him.

Ask yourself, "What exists beyond my comfort zone?" Could it be something much bigger than yourself? If you struggle with the idea or don't believe that you can succeed outside your current comfort levels, ask the Lord to show you how He sees you. Just borrow a pair of His lenses until you start to see yourself the way He fashioned you. The next time you sit down to work on your business, you need to identify the expected outcome, what is desired, and what goes beyond the current expectation. Your competition will likely only go as far as delivering, but your goal is to expand beyond and ***over-deliver*** on current expectations. There's a blessing in your hard work!

BOSS TRUTH #13

THE BEST PRODUCT YOU WILL EVER CREATE IS YOURSELF

*"You formed my inward parts;
You covered [wove] me in my mother's
womb. I will praise You, for I am
fearfully and wonderfully made;
Marvelous are Your works, And that
my soul knows very well."*
–PSALM 139:13-14

As an entrepreneur, you are your own brand. Consequently, people will buy into you first before they invest in your product. Making an impression is even more critical to your success, especially in a world filled with attention spans of nine seconds or less.[8] You stand out by allowing what you love about yourself to be reflected in your business. Great business leaders understand why they are great. They are confident in their ability to produce results in a way no one else can. The greatest business leaders spend years honing their craft, and this requires: self-discovery, self-identification, and self-mastery. As a boss, you must understand that *you* are a product. Every product has its own personality, its own audience, and its own purpose. ***You are not for everybody!*** Your brand has a specific environment in which you can flourish. However, you can't begin to take advantage of your environment until you've embraced and become ***magnified*** in your identity. You are your best product, so make sure you represent your brand well.

BOSS TRUTH #14

CREATE YOUR OWN TRIBE

"...He called them, and immediately they left the boat and their father, and followed Him. And Jesus went about all Galilee, teaching in their synagogues, preaching the gospel of the Kingdom, and healing all kinds of sickness and all kinds of disease among the people. Then His fame went throughout all Syria... Great multitudes followed Him– from Galilee, and from Decapolis, Jerusalem, Judea, and beyond the Jordan."

–MATTHEW 4:22B-24A, 25

Your tribe members are your evangelists. They share your stories, products, and services with everyone in their network. Most importantly, they buy your stuff. You can't do anything successfully without your tribe – your members, Instagram followers, Facebook friends, YouTube subscribers, etc. These are ***your*** tribe members, and you are their leader. The best companies and brands are experts at creating heart-to-heart connections and building their tribes with a focus on relationships, rather than returns. ***Tribe leaders are connection specialists.*** They always see the bigger picture. The best way to build your tribe is to offer valuable content and to be consistent. You must earn the respect of your followers through vulnerability, genuineness, and honesty.

While running a PR company, I became so used to marketing my clients that when it came time to market myself, I felt awkward. I didn't have a lot of friends or followers on any of my social media accounts, because I didn't see a need for it. When I began to realize the importance of building my own tribe, I felt a bit overwhelmed. The thought of talking to people I didn't know scared me. I felt like it would take me years to obtain thousands of followers, but it didn't. Once I overcame the fear of self-promotion (***more on that later***), and allowed people to see me for who I was, I began to attract followers because I was confident in my ability to share value. You may get on Periscope[9] and only share your value with a few viewers, and that's OK! Don't be discouraged. Don't try to be anyone else but yourself. You are enough, and there are people out there who will appreciate what you have to offer. Your tribe members will fall in love with you, follow you, and support you if you are yourself and commit to providing value.

I want you to choose three different platforms you can use to connect with and build your tribe followers. If your preference is writing, consider starting a blog. If you prefer talking, check out video platforms such as Periscope or start a podcast. Once you've selected your platforms, I want you to commit to producing content that people want to hear about at least seven times a week. The key is to keep people engaged and entertained. If you don't know what content to produce, simply ask your tribe members what they need. Produce meaningful content that adds value to a specific area of their lives.

BOSS TIP

Feeling stuck?
Download the free *Bossed Up Content Strategy Guide* to organize your ideas and stay on track to deliver consistent and valuable content to your tribe: www.tamarhuggins.com/bossedup.

NOTES

BOSS TRUTH #15

PRODUCE GREAT RESULTS

"And seeing a fig tree by the road, He came to it and found nothing on it but leaves, and said to it, 'Let no fruit grow on you ever again.' Immediately the fig tree withered away."

–MATTHEW 21:18-19

Rewards are the result of hard work. Your goal should always be to produce work that makes you feel fulfilled and that is pleasing to God. I say this very same thing to my daughter every day. It's her second rule during homework. The first is to never put yourself down, and the third is to complete the work quickly ***and*** correctly. Sometimes, we place too much emphasis on completing the work rather than producing our absolute best. The end result is that our brand suffers: we lose money and have to deal with unsatisfied customers.

There is a phrase used in carpentry that says, "Measure twice. Cut once," which means that it is better to double-check and be sure than to make careless moves. This wisdom can be applied to all industries of business. If you're going to complete a task or goal, count the cost, measure your outcomes, and execute with greatness.

Jesus cursed the fig tree that did not produce any results (***fruit***). Notice how there were branches and leaves, but still ***no fruit***. Discipline yourself and bloom fully in your business endeavors: do your work properly and don't become the fig tree. Philippians 2:13 says, "It is God who works in you both to will and to do for His good pleasure." Ask God to give you the will, strength, and encouragement to produce work He would be proud of.

BOSS TRUTH #16

BUILD AN HONORABLE REPUTATION

"A good name is to be chosen
rather than great riches,
Loving favor rather
than silver and gold."
–PROVERBS 22:1

In business, your reputation is all you have. When you work hard and produce great results, people take notice. As well, when you are dishonest or your ethics come into question, it spreads like wildfire. There is a story about a prominent man in the business community who, for years, was held in high regard because of his leadership position in a pillar organization within the community. However, those who worked with the individual often had negative things to say about his sense of entitlement and lack of professionalism. It just so happened that the individual, who is a Christian, was accused of committing fraud, and both local and national news outlets ran with the story. Not only was his reputation ruined, but also the reputation of the organization he associated with. This story is not uncommon. Sometimes when we believe we've "made it," we forget where we came from; we disregard our Godly principles and allow greed or other sins to cloud our judgments.

No amount of money can truly fix a tarnished reputation. You need humility to survive in this world of business. God will never give you more than you can handle, so don't try to take on more than you are ready for. Ask the Holy Spirit to help keep you accountable for all of your actions. Ask the Lord to reveal your potential weak spots, and pray for strength in those areas. I want you to identify your core values and develop the integrity to uphold them no matter the circumstance.

BOSS TIP

Values are the foundations that drive most, if not all, of our decisions in business and in life. Use your *Boss Journal* to write down ten or more values that are important to you. Knowing your values can provide tremendous insight into who you are. It's important to note that our values change over time, so I would advise you to revisit what you've written in the next six to twelve months.

NOTES

BOSS TRUTH #17

INCREASE YOUR NETWORK

"...Oh that you would bless me indeed, and enlarge my territory, that Your hand would be with me, and that You would keep me from evil..."
–1 CHRONICLES 4:10

In most businesses, your success is determined by three things: the results you produce, the strength of your personal brand, and the people you know. Thankfully, all three of these areas are within your control. I've already addressed work quality and personal brand, so let's look at the size of your network.

Networking starts with having a vision and a sense of purpose that is far bigger than anything we are able to achieve on our own. If I didn't have a clear vision for my business, I would not have been in the position to receive the individuals who ultimately changed my life. There were a lot of hidden gems in my extended network; some of them I met by chance or through a mutual connection.

In Genesis 40-41, we see that Joseph met the chief butler in prison, who ultimately connected him with Pharaoh. Pharaoh was greatly troubled by a dream, and no one was found among his wise men who could interpret it. It was Joseph's confidence in God and accuracy in dream interpretation that caused the butler to later remember him and mention his name. So Joseph was summoned, and his wisdom and advice were unmatched and greatly pleasing to the king. The result? Joseph became the second most powerful person in Egypt – the most influential nation on earth at that time. I believe that you have someone in your network right now who is willing and able to contribute something significant to your life's purpose. Ask God to extend your reach and influence. Pray for His guidance in connecting you with people to prosper your vision, even as you position yourself to be a prosperous help to others.

BOSS TRUTH #18

ERADICATE THE FEAR OF SELF-PROMOTION

"Let your light so shine before men, that they may see your good works and glorify your Father in heaven."
–MATTHEW 5:16

An integral part of personal branding is promoting yourself. Many of you fear self-promotion because you haven't been delivered from the thoughts and opinions of others. You fear judgment or that you won't be well-received, so you keep your achievements to yourself. I felt like this once. As I mentioned before, I am an introvert and promoting myself is not something I felt comfortable doing. I always felt like my work should speak for itself, and if I worked hard enough, people would notice. The truth is, only a few people noticed. They only heard pieces about me and didn't have enough to capture the full picture of who I was. Once I realized that I was holding myself back by not promoting myself, I began to share my value more openly with my network, and people began to notice. One of the major results of that shift was my nomination and winning the Harry Jerome Young Entrepreneur Award. This was a huge accomplishment for me. Now I am more than an entrepreneur – I am an award-winning entrepreneur.

There's nothing wrong with a little shameless plug here and there. You are your #1 client! You have to hustle and build your brand if you expect to be successful. No one is going to promote you the way you can ***and*** should promote yourself. Your intention with self-promotion should never be to show off or overshare. Be proud, and share with the intention to inspire and add value to others. Part of eradicating your fear of self-promotion is owning the feeling of confidence that results from the favour that God has shown toward you. To hide your "good works" is to hold back the greatness God has used within you to produce something worthy of recognition and celebration. Whenever you achieve something, share it! Since there is a thin line between confidence and boastfulness, ask the Holy Spirit to nudge you if the self-promotion becomes overbearing.

BOSS TRUTH #19

ONLY COMPETE WITH THE PERSON IN THE MIRROR

"And do not be conformed to this world, but be transformed by the renewing of your mind, that you may prove what is that good, and acceptable and perfect will of God."
–ROMANS 12:2

Everywhere you look, society tells you how to fit in with others. Pop culture dictates what's hot and who we should become, but what does God say? Leave room for the Lord to provide instruction because you are the only ***you*** in existence. That means that no one else can effectively prompt your path to success in the customizable way that God has destined you to succeed. Your focus should be on the one in the mirror – ***YOU***. You were born with a competitive edge, but it will remain untapped unless you break away from conformity.

I have always been the girl that ran from conformity. When others went right, I went left. When all the girls in my fourth grade class had the latest chunky heeled shoes, I was rocking my colourful Patrick Ewing sneakers. Adults always told me I was ***hard of hearing*** because I always wanted to do things my own way. Now, at 30, I still don't understand why certain people don't want to be themselves. Living a life of non-conformity has set me far above the benchmarks that others set for my life. I learned to approach challenges with wildly ambitious solutions that I am often able to implement. The result is that I am able to create meaningful impact in all the areas I operate in throughout my life.

You have to love yourself and have the guts to explore your own path. ***Be adventurous.*** There's already a million other people out there trying to be someone else on a road not conducive to their nature. Step north and partner with God to reach a success that only you can uniquely achieve.

BOSS TRUTH #20

USE YOUR TALENTS OR LOSE THEM

"For to everyone who has, more will be given, and he will have abundance; but from him who does not have, even what he has will be taken away."

—MATTHEW 25:29

The Parable of the Talents is a story about the use and underuse of gifts and talents. The parable tells us that talents were distributed "to each according to his own ability." We don't all have the same abilities, but each one of us has our own, and each one of us has a responsibility to use the abilities we have been given. The story begins with a man who was given five talents – he worked with what he had, used them all, and gained five more. Likewise, the man with only two talents worked with the little he had and gained two more talents. Lastly, there was a man who was given one talent, and did absolutely nothing with it. The servant's master was upset with the one-talent man, not because he didn't develop as many talents as the others, but because he had done nothing with what he was given. As a result, his talent was taken away and given to the man with five talents.

I believe you have amazing gifts inside you, but some are afraid to explore and add to them because of the fear of failure. Some people compare themselves to others who are multi-talented and are convinced they can never be like them. The truth is, the Lord will never expect you to do more than what you are able – only to do the best with what He has given you. If you have that one thing going for you, ***work it like nobody's business.***

BOSS CHALLENGE #2

Complete the *Bossed Up Self-Assessment*, which you can find at www.tamarhuggins.com/bossedup, to identify the ingredients in your special sauce. What makes you fascinating? Discover what your spiritual giftings are, and uncover their natural meaning.

CHAPTER 3

PASSION

BOSS TRUTH #21

EXPLORE YOUR PAIN POINTS

"But to each one of us grace was given according to the measure of Christ's gift."
–EPHESIANS 4:7

A Bishop once told me, "Whatever troubles your heart is the key to identifying your passion." A few years ago, one of my high school teachers asked me and three other ladies to be guest a speaker at a town hall meeting for teen girls. As is often the case when I talk to groups of young adults, they listen intently but don't engage in conversation until they have a private moment with me. One student confided that she was a teenage mom on social assistance, and she was desperately looking for a job to support herself and her child. She felt that the school system had given up on her, and she felt alone. My heart wept for her. I sympathized with her situation and vowed to make myself available to mentor and help her with whatever she needed.

A seed was planted within me during my experience with this young girl. I realized that watching young people suffer or fail in life was a huge pain point for me. My interaction with her made me realize what my passion was, and I made it my life's mission to support the young people who others had given up on. In Ephesians 4:7, we learn that we are each graced with a gift from Christ, and it's specifically measured for each of us. We are to use these gifts to help others, and I realized this particular passion was an area where I could pour out my gifts. Now I use my passion for entrepreneurship to educate others on how to make a living by doing what they love. I also use my natural ability to inspire others to see the greatness that God has placed within them. What does your pain point tell you about your passion?

BOSS TIP

Search yourself and identify the pain points you feel in your heart. Use your *Boss Journal* to organize your thoughts and feelings. Dig deep here.
Ask the Holy Spirit for revelation and confirmation in the area of your passion.
Allow the Holy Spirit to guide you toward the one pain point you should explore as a potential business idea.

NOTES

BOSS TRUTH #22

RESURRECT YOUR DEAD DREAMS

"Again He said unto me, Prophesy to these bones, and say to them, O dry bones, hear the word of the Lord! Thus says the Lord God to these bones: Surely I will cause breath to enter into you, and you shall live."
–EZEKIEL 37:4-5

As a child, I had dreams of becoming a singer. I wanted to be famous like my favourite singer Brandy Norwood. The truth is, I couldn't sing, ***and*** I was super shy. However, that didn't stop me from dreaming about the possibilities! Many of us had wild ambitions and dreams that exceeded the heights of the sky when we were children. Then, at some point, our wings were clipped, and we no longer soared as we once did. We grew up, but we packed our dreams deep inside us.

Think about where you would be if you were living your life's dream right now. Would you be happier? More fulfilled? I believe God cares about our sense of wonder and preserving our ability to dream – ***and to dream big.*** He wants us to search our hearts and reignite the desires He naturally placed inside us. Whether you always saw yourself helping people, being famous, or owning your own establishment, revisit your dreams. Our dreams are supposed to sharpen and mature as they come to fruition – not become stifled by the cares of life and circumstances.

The Word of God shows how we can speak to the dry bones in our lives. We have the God-given authority to command the dry areas of our lives to live again, and He will breathe life into them! Test the Word of God and speak to those dry bones right now. It doesn't matter how old you are now, trust and believe your dreams can come alive again. I want you to read and meditate on Ezekiel 37:1-14. Search your heart, and ask the Holy Spirit to confirm the dream you allowed to die, so that it can be resurrected.

Revisit and expand. As a child, you may have seen your dream in its simplest form. Now, it's time for you to expand it. How big could it be today? How can it fit into the context of how God uses you?

Please note: Resurrecting a dead dream doesn't mean you stop doing the will of God in one area to do something else. You can give glory to the Lord through many different avenues!

BOSS TRUTH #23

GOD FULFILLS OUR HEART'S DESIRES

"Delight yourself also in the Lord,
And He shall give you
the desires of your heart."
–PSALM 37:4

Desire is the starting point of achievement. In order to achieve anything, you have to want it ***bad***. Scripture tells us that we must desire the things of God more than our own earthly desires. So when we seek to please God, He in turn grants us the desires of our heart (because our intentions have aligned with His). This is part of the fulfilled life we have access to as children of God. As we seek to honor God's will, He pours back into us the endowment to maximize our potential in using our gifts to serve others.

You have to be very specific about what it is that you want, because God doesn't operate in confusion. If you want to make a million dollars next year, great! Map out how you want to achieve it. Identify every single step you need to take to make it happen. If you are selling a product, decide how much you have to sell and by what date in order to reach your goal. Next, identify what you are willing to sacrifice to achieve your goals. God will bless you according to the seeds you have planted, but if you make a request and do nothing but sit with your palms up, you'll forfeit your harvest. You can achieve anything you think of through Jesus Christ, but what you obtain is only limited by your own actions.

Ecclesiastes 11:6 says, "In the morning sow your seed, And in the evening do not withhold your hand; For you do not know which will prosper, Either this or that..." This means that we are to take advantage of every opportunity because, as we plant and sow into our goals, certain efforts may cause us to reap in different ways. Therefore, as you pursue your desires, strategize and try different things to figure out what prospers...but doing nothing is not an option.

BOSS TIP

Use your *Boss Journal* to write out the desires of your heart and the sacrifices you will make to achieve them. Revisit your journal daily to keep yourself accountable.

NOTES

BOSS TRUTH #24

YOU CAN SERVE GOD BY DOING WHAT YOU LOVE

*"You shall love the Lord your God
with all your heart, with all your soul,
and with all your mind."*
– MATTHEW 22:37

Picture this: you have this flame burning in your heart, and you can't sleep or think about anything other than this one idea. On the other hand, you feel conflicted because you think the work you want to do doesn't have anything to do with glorifying God. Do you pursue it?

A friend of mine shared an idea for a business he wanted to create that would encourage and manage mentor and mentee relationships. He told me, "I finally feel like I'm doing work for God. I've felt so guilty working all these years because I didn't feel like I was honoring God." I told him, "First of all, you need to change your view of what doing God's work looks like." Often, we think we can only honor God through charitable work centered around the church. This couldn't be farther from the truth! When we are aligned with God, He can be glorified wherever we take Him and with whatever He's given us. We put ***our own*** limits on what we can do, but Jesus says ***we are to do greater works***.[10] He said we are to heal the sick, raise the dead, and cast out demons. Sounds a bit crazy right? Now shift your thinking a bit.

Perhaps you are called to heal those who are financially sick and drowning in debt, or to inspire and raise the spiritually dead who feel they can no longer go on in life. You might also be called to free and deliver the oppressed through counseling or mentorship. As Holy Spirit-filled believers, healing, resurrection, and deliverance are our portions, but they are not limited to just working directly in the church. It is possible to accomplish God's work through entrepreneurship – you just have to engage with the Holy Spirit who helps us think creatively. The possibilities are limited only by your own imagination. Pray for the revelation of His will and a heart of obedience to walk in it.

BOSS TRUTH #25

YOU CAN MAKE MONEY DOING WHAT YOU LOVE

"Beloved, I pray that you may prosper in all things and be in health, just as your soul prospers."
–3 JOHN 1:2

Who said you can't make money doing what you love? Only discontented, unfulfilled people tell you what you ***can't*** achieve, and it's because they are too scared to achieve success for themselves. There is a misconception that passions don't make money or that it has to be "something you do on the side." This is a lie from the pits of hell. You have to begin looking at your passion as one that ***can*** turn into a profitable business. Take nonprofits and charities for example. Many nonprofits fail, not because of lack of passion, but rather the failure to see the organization as a business.

I want you to write down three things you are deeply passionate about. Rank your interest level for each item. Then, map out seven ways you can generate income from each of your passion items. If you get stuck, research the industry to see how other entrepreneurs are generating income. After that, pray and ask the Holy Spirit to confirm the revenue streams that are right for your business. Strategize demographics and explore contexts that would allow your passions to flow. Remove the restrictions from your mind, and get creative.

The fact is, many people do what they love and are successful at it. I am a living testament to that. If you don't think you can be successful doing what you love, then you have to shift your mindset. You must view passion as the conduit – ***not the consequence*** – of your financial success. God doesn't want you to be broke, and He doesn't expect you to do His work without money. In the previous focus scripture, the Apostle John speaks a prosperous blessing toward Gaius, one who has been found walking in the truth of God. Claim prosperity for yourself! Let that be a focal point in your prayer life, because if your passion aligns with His will for you, ***trust and believe*** that financial success is attached to it!

BOSS TRUTH #26

YOU MAY HAVE TO REIGNITE THE FLAME

"He will baptize you with the Holy Spirit and fire."
–LUKE 3:16B

Let's face it, sometimes passion dies down. There will come a time when you have to remind yourself of your ***why*** – why you started, why you endure, and why you must finish. Along the way, people may try to force you in another direction, you might become discouraged, or you might end up facing the decision of compromising your vision strictly for financial gain. I've questioned myself countless times during my seven-year career as an entrepreneur. Self-doubt would begin to creep in when things weren't going right. I thought, ***maybe I'm not supposed to do this***. Then, right before I felt like giving up, I would hear an encouraging word from God that recharged my spirit. He would often use a close friend to remind me that He is in control, and that I am indeed on the right path.

For example, I went through two years of consistently being denied startup capital. It's difficult to progress in your business without money, right? That was a tough season, and it made me question whether I was in the right business. Then, the Lord reminded me that He doesn't expect me to serve His people broke and that my breakthrough was right around the corner. My breakthrough came in 2013 when I learned that my nonprofit was awarded $50,000 for a very competitive grant application I submitted. I really had to prove that my business idea was sustainable and socially impactful all at the same time. My idea to train next generation tech leaders wasn't like anything the funders had ever supported, but when God gives you favour with men, unusual things happen! He strategically placed an individual on the grant review committee who supported my initiative from day one. I believe that if it wasn't for this one person, the funders would have never taken a chance with my idea. But – that's God! He's always working behind the scenes in our favour.

I've learned that we are to be "fervent in spirit."[11] Fervency is passionate intensity – a burning zeal for that which we long for. When you begin to feel the fire you once had for your business dying down, evaluate why this is happening. Could it be that you've allowed frustrations or lack of progression to get to you? Or, could it be that you are losing touch with your original goals? In that case, you need to take some time out to recharge and remind yourself why you started. Identify what is stopping you from moving forward, and create steps to overcome those barriers. Furthermore, take some time out to reflect on your ***why***. You can do this weekly, monthly, or quarterly. Be honest about how you feel at that very moment and journal it, or share it with your team. Be sure to note all of your challenges and victories so that you can refer back to them when you need to be reminded of your ***why***.

NOTES

BOSS TRUTH #27

PASSION CREATES GREATER IMPACT

"...the Lord has sought for Himself a man after His own heart, and the Lord has commanded Him to be commander over His people..."
–1 SAMUEL 13:14

King David was unarguably the most passionate warrior and ruler over all of Israel. Above all else, he was passionate about God – even more than riches and recognition. Through the power of God, David became tremendously victorious at a very young age, and the fame grew when he fought and killed Goliath.[12] The David that was king was the same David that was a shepherd. He tended pastures just as honorably and passionately as he did God's Kingdom. David's actions revolutionized how we see worship, even unto this day. He made praise and repentance the standard and shook nations with a humble heart. The only way he accomplished these things was being great privately before God exalted him publicly.

My favourite and most impactful historical events include the Civil Rights Movement led by Dr. King, the Black Power Movement led by Malcolm X, and the Black Panthers. ***They were all fueled by passion***. We can create greater impact with the work we do when we do it passionately. Passion comes from the heart. Passion is what gives us the strength and confidence to walk boldly in the face of adversity. It is also what brings us closer to victory and allows us to create not only greater impact, but ***lasting*** impact in the world. Only passion can create ripple effects that endure throughout the years ***or even generations***.

BOSS TRUTH #28

COMMIT TO YOUR PASSION

"Commit your works to the Lord,
And your thoughts [plans]
will be established."
–PROVERBS 16:3

Once you've identified what you are passionate about, you must commit to it. There are entrepreneurs who make their money by flip-flopping and jumping on whatever is hot at the time. They never commit to a single goal because money is their god. As God-based entrepreneurs, money should not be our end goal; everything we do is to bring honor and glory to God's Kingdom. You may find yourself working on multiple projects at one time, but just remember that everything you do now is a stepping stone to something much greater.

You now have a responsibility to yourself and to God. It's good to evaluate what that responsibility looks like as your business and your goals evolve. Remain focused and remember there is purpose in your work. Also, do not depend on anyone to hold you accountable for the things you said you would get done – you must ***make yourself*** accountable. Many people commit to getting things done, but it never happens. You are not one of those people. Get the work done, by any means necessary.

BOSS TRUTH #29

YOUR PASSION IS CONNECTED TO YOUR ABILITIES

—

"As each one has received a gift, minister it to one another, as good stewards of the manifold grace of God. If anyone speaks, let him speak as the oracles [utterances] of God. If anyone ministers, let him do it as with the ability which God supplies…"

–1 PETER 4:10-11A

Nehemiah is a prime example of how God can use the abilities and resources of just one person to change an entire city. On the outside, he was the cupbearer of the king. However, there were abilities within him that would allow him to accomplish a task that was bigger than himself. After hearing of how his ancestral city, Jerusalem, was in ruins, he began to weep. Nehemiah fasted and prayed for God to show him favor with the king, that he might return and rebuild the city walls and restore the people to a place of honor. According to "the good hand of God that was upon him,"[13] his request was granted. Furthermore, he was given horsemen, captains, decrees for safe passage, and permits to acquire building materials. As the work commenced, he faced tremendous opposition, burdens, and threats, but his response to each one was that they would prevail and that God would destroy the plans of their enemies. It took only ***fifty-two days*** to rebuild Jerusalem. Nehemiah not only restored honor to the physical aspects of the city, but he also reestablished God's ordinances and reverence within the hearts of the people. Nehemiah was brave and had a natural ability to pioneer a movement and bring restoration through great leadership, courage, strategy, and determination.

There is a powerful statement by Bob Sorge, author of ***Secrets of the Secret Place***, where he says, "God wants to walk with us before He works through us. So He will wait to act until He finds the right man or woman through whom He can work."[14] There's something mighty to be done for the Kingdom, and God is waiting on you. As you seek to be good stewards over the abilities and skills you've been given, I want you to ask yourself: What problems do I hold the solution to? What drives me to take action? What does "action" look like for me?

When you seek God's will for your life, your passion and skills will naturally connect, because each of us are called by God to minister to others in a special way. Entrepreneurship is a venture in which God works through our inner passions and innate abilities to accomplish many goals related to the Kingdom. Entrepreneurship is our vocation. Vocation is taken from the Latin word ***voca,*** which means ***inner voice***. Every one of us has an identifiable voice deep within, as well as abilities and skill sets that are complementary to the call of God on our lives. Once we recognize what these are, we can accomplish anything.

BOSS TIP

Create a list of things you are passionate about. Then list your identified skills or abilities. You should begin to see a connection between your passions and abilities. This will help you develop a clear picture of how you can use your God-given abilities to work in an area you are passionate about.

NOTES

BOSS TRUTH #30

BUILD PEOPLE UP, DON'T TEAR THEM DOWN

"Therefore let us pursue the things which make for peace and the things by which one may edify another."
–ROMANS 14:19

As you build your way to becoming your own boss, recognize your positive qualities, ***as well as those that have the potential to make you a nightmare as a boss***. As I mentioned in the introduction, I have definitely encountered these "soulless leaders" before, and it has made me more conscious of my own leadership style. After college, I landed a job at one of the most creative ad agencies in Toronto. For the first few months of being there, I had a very inspiring boss. After a short while, she moved to another company. I was hurt because she was so special to me. She gave me responsibilities that no one in my role was technically allowed to have. She was such an encouragement to me, and she saw my true potential. The managers that came after her stripped me of my responsibilities and beat me down into a box. They made me question my own abilities, sabotaged my work, and made me feel like an outcast.

God revealed that I was under a spiritual attack, as the spirit of Jezebel was operating in the women in the department. The spirit of Jezebel manifests as overbearing, controlling, and destructive. I felt physically ill, and due to the heavy stress I was under, my hair began to fall out, ***and*** my personal relationships suffered. Perseverance was how I was able to make it through to the end. I lost my job during the recession, but ***it was a huge blessing for me***. It was at this point that I started my PR company and landed award-winning media personalities and athletes as clients! During this transition, I learned that the right leader has the ability to catapult their individual team members to be someone great, but a contentious, hard-hearted leader can do exactly the opposite – rob you of your joy and drive, and eventually kill your passion. I vowed to never be like the horrible leaders in my past, because I knew firsthand how badly somebody's self-confidence could suffer, as mine did. I want you to be the kind of leader who enhances the lives of those you lead through the pursuit of peace and those things that build people up, not tear them down. Have authority and be assertive, but just don't drag people through the mud while doing it.

BOSS CHALLENGE #3

Over the next five days, participate in the *Passion-to-Profit* challenge to identify how to use your passion to generate seven sources of income. Visit www.tamarhuggins.com/bossedup to access the challenge.

NOTES

CHAPTER 4

EMPOWERMENT

BOSS TRUTH #31

BELIEVE YOU ARE QUALIFIED

"I will make you a great nation; I will bless you and make your name great; And you shall be a blessing."
–GENESIS 12:2

Before you launch your business or even share your ideas with anyone, you must already believe you can accomplish the goal you've set for yourself. When you begin to share your ideas with people, don't be surprised if certain individuals question your ability or authority. Some people may have their intention in the right place when they question you, and some are simply going to hate. If you or your idea aren't strong enough to withstand negativity, you will begin to question yourself, your qualifications, and God! If God called you to do it, then you already have what it takes to get it done, ***period***.

The exercises in previous chapters taught you how to seek God for clarity, and help you explore your passions and connect them with your natural abilities. At this point, you should feel your confidence rising. It is your spiritual inheritance to succeed[15]. When you are questioned about your ability to do what God has already qualified you for, I want you to stand firm and speak boldly. It's not about trying to convince others. It's about owning your purpose! Each time you speak your truth, you will begin to own it, and you will begin to care less and less about what others think you can and can't do. Learn to move forward with style and grace because your confidence is in God.

BOSS TRUTH #32

INVEST IN YOURSELF

*"The heart of the prudent acquires knowledge,
And the ear of the wise seeks knowledge."*
–PROVERBS 18:15

Y***ou*** are the most profitable investment to your future. You cannot expect anyone to invest in you or your business if you haven't first invested in yourself. Every little bit counts! Because God has given you many talents, He expects you to invest time improving on what He's given you...***and even acquiring more.*** You might be thinking ***I don't have time to go back to school***. Well, no one is saying you have to become a full-time or part-time college student. What I'm saying is that you have to find ways to sharpen and build upon the skills you already have in order for progression and growth to happen in your business. You have to commit yourself to learning.

This might mean taking time off to attend a three-day conference to learn about new industry trends or committing yourself to read one book a week. The easiest way for me to learn is to simply pick up a book and read it. I am always amazed when I hear people call themselves an expert in any particular area, yet they haven't even read any literature on the subject. These are also the same type of people who seem to have advice for everyone else ***but*** themselves. Invest in yourself first. Don't expect anyone to do it for you. Be willing to work for everything.

BOSS TRUTH #33

YOU HAVE THE AUTHORITY TO SPEAK YOUR SUCCESS INTO EXISTENCE

"Have faith in God. For assuredly,
I say to you, whoever says to this mountain, '
Be removed and cast into the sea,' and does
not doubt in his heart, but believes
that those things he says will be done,
he will have whatever he says."
–MARK 11:22-23

A declaration is a very explicit statement or announcement. When we make daily declarations about our lives and businesses, it puts our underlying purpose into action. When you declare something, you mark it with God's intentions with authority through Jesus Christ. When Jesus cursed the fig tree, His command wasn't just against a tree, but against unfruitfulness. His declaration against it correlates with the principle of John 15:1-8, which states, "Every branch in Me [Jesus] that does not bear fruit, He [God] takes away..." With His declaration, He put into motion a principle of God's Kingdom. This shows that it is ***our faith*** coupled with ***His truth*** that makes our declarations powerful and edifying.

Your daily declarations are important and should embody your ***why*** (which you explored in chapter 3). Here are some great examples of declarations you can begin using in your life right now:

* "I bless others and bring joy into the lives of others through my business; therefore, God will bless me, and I will find joy in my work."[16]
* "God has given me the ability to create abundant wealth through my business."[17]
* "My business functions using Kingdom principles above the economies of this world."[18]

Your declaration should clearly state what you want to happen in your business and what God has promised concerning it. Remember, when it's His will, whatever you speak into the atmosphere must come to pass.

BOSS TIP

Use the notes section to develop daily decrees and declare them every day!

NOTES

BOSS TRUTH #34

CHECK YOUR EGO AT THE DOOR

"When pride comes,
then comes shame;
But with the humble is wisdom."
–PROVERBS 11:2

I've talked to you about confidence, qualification, and validation. However, for some of us, there comes a time when there is an imbalance. For example, God blesses a person, and they forget where He's brought them from prior to the blessing. Do you remember your humble beginnings? I remember when I didn't have a dime in my bank account and had to ask a friend for money to put gas in my car. I know that without humbleness, God can bring me right back there in a second.

Have you ever wondered why shame comes with pride? It's because pride blinds us, so we end up embarrassing ourselves. It hinders us from perceiving the fullness of what God wants to do, either in us or in the people around us. Wisdom is an attribute of a humble person, because a humble heart is an open heart. Therefore, wisdom can dwell in our hearts because wisdom doesn't claim to know everything.

Don't allow your ego to get to a point where God has to humble you. Instead, ***choose*** the humble and wise way first. One of the ways you can tell your ego is outgrowing your reality is how you react to advice or counsel. When people ***you trust*** advise you in different circumstances or scenarios about your character but you continue to ignore it, you could have an issue with your ego. Even if you don't agree with it, don't stay offended. You have a responsibility to seek clarity in prayer and see what causes people to perceive you the way they do. The quickest answered prayers come when we ask God about our character.

There is no better way to stay humble than to give up your time to help others less fortunate than you. Commit some of your personal time to serving, whether it's through mentoring inner-city youth or distributing socks to the homeless during the winter. Keep in mind 1 Timothy 6:17-18, which says, "Command those who are rich in this present age not to be haughty, nor to trust in uncertain riches but in the living God, who gives us richly all things to enjoy. Let them do good, that they be rich in good works, ready to give, willing to share."

BOSS TRUTH #35

POWER IS HAVING THE OPTION TO SAY NO

"...let it be known to you,
O king, that we do not serve your
gods, nor will we worship the gold
image which you have set up."
–DANIEL 3:18

I recently attended a Bible study class on ungodly soul ties, and I came to understand how the principle applies to business partnerships in addition to relationships. Everything that glitters really isn't gold. A lot of successful business people dabble in the occult to obtain success and wealth. Out of concern, one night a friend reached out to tell me that her educational institution was led by a woman who was a self-proclaimed witch. I expressed the dangers of continuing her involvement with the school and told her to cut ties immediately. I prayed with my friend and taught her how to rebuke the spirit of witchcraft, and break any soul tie that was made. She was scared, but I reassured her that God had her back.

You will hear many successful entrepreneurs give praise to other entities, such as the universe, for their success. In Romans 1:25 it reads, "...who exchanged the truth of God for the lie, and worshiped and served the creature rather than the Creator..." The universe is not God. If I don't hear someone acknowledge God, I would seriously question where they are obtaining their success from. I am not ashamed to acknowledge God as my one and only source of success. God is the CEO of my life, ***period.*** Just like Shadrach, Meshach, and Abednego refused to bow to Nebuchadnezzar's false gods and gold images,[19] we should be willing to say "No" to the evil temptations we face as Christian entrepreneurs. If a business partnership seems too good to be true, ask questions. Think of business relationships like personal relationships. Would you invest time and energy into someone you didn't truly know?

No amount of money is worth your representation of Christ. The consequence of these soul ties are open doorways that give the enemy legal grounds to attack your business, personal finances, and even your health. Here are some signs to identify if you've created an unholy soul tie with an individual or company:

1. The individual/company dabbles in the occult (consults with psychics, mediums, practices witchcraft).

2. The individual/company follows religious practices contrary to the belief of God, Jesus Christ, and the Holy Spirit (i.e. praises the universe for their success).

3. The individual/company wants you to sign anything in blood, join a secret society, or otherwise enter into an unholy agreement that goes beyond standard legal agreements.

If you find yourself in a partnership that is ungodly, it's not too late to cut the ties. If you are unsure, pray that God gives you a supernatural dose of discernment. Then, ask the Holy Spirit to provide you with the strategy to break the soul tie, and walk away from the partnership.

BOSS TIP

Get specific with your prayers.
Visit www.tamarhuggins.com/bossedup to download spiritual warfare prayers designed specifically for entrepreneurs.

NOTES

BOSS TRUTH #36

STUDY TO SHOW YOURSELF APPROVED

"Be diligent [study] to present yourself approved to God, a worker who does not need to be ashamed, rightly dividing the word of truth."
–2 TIMOTHY 2:15

Studying the Word of God is an important part of your spiritual development. When I study and memorize God's word, I feel equipped when I need to face challenges or adversity. Whenever I need confidence in my financial stability, I recite Philippians 4:19, ***"And my God shall supply all your need according to His riches in glory by Christ Jesus."*** Before I ask a potential corporate sponsor or funder for money, I quote Proverbs 3:4, ***"So find favor and high esteem [good understanding] In the sight of God and man."***

The Word of God says that even Jesus grew in wisdom and maturity. It also says that He increased in favor with God and men.[20] This means that He submitted Himself to knowledge from others and even from the scripture texts that were available then. It also shows that even though He was the Son of God, He still went through processes of establishing relationships among people, gaining trust, learning the ways of God, and discovering how He was to change the world. Through the busyness of getting products to customers, hiring new staff, and traveling around the world, there has to be a set time for studying the Word of God. It should be continuous and made a priority because it is pivotal to the success of your entire life.

BOSS TIP

Use your *Boss Journal* to create a list of scriptures that strengthen and motivate you. Quote them daily until you memorize and can recite them in your time of need.

BOSS TRUTH #37

CONQUER YOUR MOUNTAINS

"...assuredly, I say to you,
if you have faith as a mustard seed,
you will say to this mountain,
'Move from here to there,'
and it will move."
–MATTHEW 17:20

As children of God, we are called to be the salt and light of the earth.[21] In Johnny Enlow's book ***The Seven Mountains Prophecy***, he says that the children of God should conquer the seven cultural mountains that shape our society. They are: business, arts and entertainment, education, family, government, media, and religion. Many people believe that God's work can only be done in full-time ministry. But the truth is, much of God's work can and should be done outside of the church.

The metaphorical mountains spoken of in the Bible are obstacles or high places that are seemingly impossible to conquer. Jesus proclaims that mountains are overcome by our faith, and when it comes to demonic oppression, by prayer and fasting. You may ask, "How do I conquer the mountains in my way?" Or better yet, "***Why*** should I conquer the mountains?" The answer is simple: Satan has way too much control over the mediums and institutions that shape our culture. In order to see positive change, we need to take them back. We see proof of this in the perversion of music and art, the removal of Christ from schools, and businesses that use occult practices to gain fame and wealth. In order to regain influence, we must reclaim the power.[22]

Imagine what our world would look like if corporate greed was replaced with social impact missions to revive the poor and destitute, or if corporations stopped selling cancer-causing foods and instead invested in locally-grown organic produce (which could significantly decrease the health epidemic). There are so many underutilized opportunities for us to receive creative problem-solving revelation from God. We just have to continually submit the influence we've been given to Him. As businesswomen and businessmen of God, we can reclaim the mountain of business from the enemy by:

1. Using Godly principles to guide our decision making, rather than worldly principles.
2. Choosing to openly honor God and serve others.
3. Utilizing the ***power*** of God's Kingdom through our natural and supernatural gifts.

As entrepreneurs, we must think and behave like agents of change if we want to improve the world we live in. You are already qualified and validated by God, and you have been given the authority to administer the Kingdom ***wherever you go***. Remember that!

NOTES

BOSS TRUTH #38

STAY IN THE COMPANY OF EXTRAORDINARY PEOPLE

"Now so it was that after three days they found Him in the temple, sitting in the midst of the teachers, both listening to them and asking them questions. And all who heard Him were astonished at His understanding and answers."
–LUKE 2:46-47

A great teacher of mine once said, "Pay anything to stay in the company of extraordinary people." Now, she didn't mean this in the literal sense only, although it very well could apply. You can't expect to grow and move forward surrounded by people with the same level of experience and intelligence as your own. Proverbs 13:20 tells us those who walk with the wise ***will become*** wise. Even Jesus understood this at a very young age. His parents looked for Him for ***three days***, and despite their worry and anxiety, He was completely unbothered and focused. He stated, "Why did you seek Me? Did you not know that I must be about My Father's business?" I always laugh to myself when I read this part, because I know had I said something like that to my parents, it wouldn't have ended well for me! But Jesus had a mission to accomplish, a Kingdom to transform by invading earth with the power of Heaven, and He was getting prepared to do it!

You must be strategic in your approach to gain the attention of someone who can take you to the next level. Think wildly for a minute. Who do you admire the most as a success in your industry? If you could have coffee with them for thirty minutes, I bet you'd do it! Consider how willing you would be if that person lived outside of the country. Would you purchase a plane ticket to have their undivided attention for one hour? If you answered no, you aren't ready for growth. If you said yes, ***congratulations*** – you understand the value of being in the company of someone extraordinary. You have something awesome to accomplish, just like Jesus did, and I want you to stay that hungry ***forever***. Hunger and determination remove the lid of possibilities. They are what separates you from mediocrity and complacency.

BOSS TRUTH #39

DO NOT ABUSE YOUR POWER

"Therefore, O king, let my advice be acceptable to you; break off your sins by being righteous, and [break off] your iniquities by showing mercy to the poor. Perhaps there may be a lengthening of your prosperity."

–DANIEL 4:27

These were Daniel's last words to King Nebuchadnezzar before God stripped the king of his Kingdom for seven years. Even though he had experiences with God's power through the character and interpretations of Daniel, the Word of God says that "his heart was lifted up, and his spirit was hardened in pride."[23] Because of this, the king lost his mind, and he lived and even ate among wild animals for seven years! His authority was one of the greatest given on the earth, but how God made an example out of him shows that those with power are still entrusted with a certain responsibility to walk in consideration of those under them. In the Bible, we also learn about other abusive power-hungry individuals who met their demise including Pharaoh, who used slaves for excessive physical labour. Then there was Jezebel, who used manipulation and terror to achieve her wicked means.

In business, abuse of power can take on many forms, both big and small. When people hear that term, they think of large-scale white-collar criminals down to employers pushing the working of twelve-hour shifts without breaks. Abuse of power also looks like: stealing money from your company, taking unfair advantage of free labour, and writing false charitable receipts for money. Be good stewards over what God has given you, or you run the risk of losing everything. We are to ***be*** the pattern and model of good works,[24] having integrity. Those who understand power know they don't have to abuse it to achieve what they want. Instead, they use power with wisdom to accomplish their goals. Don't reap the corrupt benefits of a crooked lifestyle. Proverbs 10:9 says, "He who walks with integrity walks securely, But he who perverts his ways will become known." Consider those God had to humble and make examples out of, and make the choice today to do business in an honorable way.

BOSS TRUTH #40

MAINTAIN YOUR AUTHORITY

"Let every soul be subject
to the governing authorities.
For there is no authority except from
God, and the authorities that exist
are appointed by God."
–ROMANS 13:1

As a young, black female working in an industry dominated by older men of other ethnicities, my authority was questioned many times. And, I've had to check people ***many times***. I encountered a tricky situation when I had to address a culturally sensitive issue between one of my staff and a staff member from a partnering organization. What made the situation tricky was how to make our partner (who is a well-known political figure) aware of the issue involving their staff. I also faced challenges from the same individual who, in my opinion, felt threatened by my authority as a woman young enough to be their child. I felt there was a spirit of contention in operation so I immediately rebuked the spirit in prayer and received the confidence I needed to address the issue. I politely let them know that if our relationship was to continue, my staff would need to be respected, period. After that, there was a shift in the atmosphere as the Holy Spirit brought in peace and harmony. In the end, everyone was getting along as though the issue had never happened.

Maintaining authority and gaining respect is not about being a ***B,*** but as a boss, it's important for people to respect your authority. The Word of God tells us that authority is given by Him – whether it's the governing authority of a country or that of an office or business. When you realize how God views order and honor, you'll have no problem exercising the power He has given you. You are not responsible for what people think or how they respond. However, if there's a job to be done and He's appointed you to lead, you ***are*** held accountable for your words and actions as it relates to truth and excellence. You have to expect that people will challenge your position at some point (or at many points) during your career. You need to have a high level of confidence, knowledge, and credibility to be able to address these challenges. Do not be afraid to put people in their place, but do it with style and grace.

BOSS CHALLENGE #4

Use your *Boss Journal* to list your weaknesses as a boss. Is it hard for you to correct your staff? Have you abused your power in any way? Being respected doesn't require you to be rude. Fast and pray about your role and responsibilities as a leader. Then, list five ways to gain the respect of your staff without being disrespectful or condescending. Practice these methods with your staff and adjust them as needed. Make note of your adjustments in your journal.

NOTES

CHAPTER 5

PURPOSE

BOSS TRUTH #41

FOLLOW THE CALLING NOT THE CROWD

"He did not do many mighty works there because of their unbelief."
–MATTHEW 13:58

God always calls us to walk the path less traveled. When Jesus walked this earth, He trail-blazed a path for us all to follow. In a society diluted by man-made religious doctrine and bureaucracy, He went against the grain to do ***His*** Father's work. He was scrutinized, and challenged everywhere He went. Still, at the end of it all, God was pleased with His Son's work.

One of the more personal difficulties that Jesus faced was being criticized by those in ***His own*** country. When they heard Him teach, they asked questions such as: "Where did this Man get this wisdom and these mighty works? Is this not the carpenter's son? Is not His mother called Mary?" They were amazed at what he taught, but they still didn't accept ***Him***. They failed to see that His anointing was from Heaven and not the works of man, so Jesus had to move on. It might have seemed more logical for Jesus to stick around to try to convince them, but ***that would have compromised His calling***. You can't please everyone, and you weren't made for everyone's acceptance. You have to **go** where God is calling you and **be** who He's made you to be.

In my case, I decided to become an entrepreneur before it was really trendy. It was a scary thought to take everything into my own hands. My financial stability, reputation, and peace of mind were solely ***my*** responsibility. Walking away from the comforts of a nine to five is a huge decision, and it was one that many didn't understand or even support, yet I did it because I knew I was built for entrepreneurship. It's not easy to be unpopular or to have the ones you love constantly question your life's purpose, but the world remembers those individuals who took risks, who were fearless and formidable. No one ever remembers the conformist who was too afraid to be different if it meant losing social acceptance. In a world where everyone wants to be the most popular person in the room, remember to stand out and follow your calling, not the crowd.

BOSS TRUTH #42

ALWAYS SEEK REVELATION FROM GOD

"...that the God of our Lord Jesus Christ, the Father of glory, may give to you the spirit of wisdom and revelation in the knowledge of Him, the eyes of your understanding being enlightened; that you may know what is the hope of His calling, what are the riches of the glory of His inheritance in the saints, and what is the exceeding greatness of His power toward us who believe..."
–EPHESIANS 1:17-19A

One of the most powerful things you can ask the Lord to do is reveal His will for you in a way you will understand. This is how we allow the wisdom from above[25] to work in our lives and business. Personally, whenever I need clarity or answers, I pray for the answer to be revealed to me during my personal prayer time with God or through a dream. When I wake up in the morning, I immediately write my dreams down and ask the Holy Spirit to clarify anything I am unsure of. God is not a genie; however, He does desire to speak and prove Himself to us. He reveals His will to us through dreams, visions, internal knowings, angels, miracles, natural occurrences, prophetic words/acts, and sometimes His audible voice. The list could go on and on because He is infinite, and although **we** are not, He has given us the ability to know Him. Proverbs 8:17 says, "I love those who love Me, and those who seek Me diligently will find Me."

Even though you can ask God to reveal or confirm anything to you (let's say a new business idea you want to pursue, but don't know how or when), the key is to be very specific about what it is you want to know. ***He cares about the details.*** God will show you things in the Spirit, and the Holy Spirit will help you translate what you've been shown into a natural execution strategy. For example, I made up in my mind that I wanted to launch this book in November during Entrepreneurship Week (a yearly event inspiring individuals to engage in entrepreneurial activities). It makes sense right? But something didn't feel right inside. Nothing was going as planned. When I realized I didn't even ask God when ***He*** wanted me to launch the book, I dropped everything, took a step back, and got on my knees in prayer. Thankfully, He responded instantly with the launch date ***and*** how I was to market the book. As I began to execute according to His strategy, everything worked out seamlessly. For your strategy, God may send someone to you to confirm what He's said. It could be a simple conversation or maybe even an encounter with a stranger. Once you pray, you must keep both your natural and spiritual eyes and ears open. Remain diligent in prayer and expect a response.

BOSS TRUTH #43

PRACTICE LISTENING

"When He, the Spirit of truth, has come, He will guide you into all truth; for He will not speak on His own authority, but whatever He hears He will speak; and He will tell you things to come. He will glorify Me [Jesus], for He will take of what is Mine and declare it to you."

–JOHN 16:13-14

Now that you've prayed and asked for revelation, you have to listen for God's voice. Listening in the Spirit means being able to identify the voice of God. God speaks to us daily. However, due to the noise of the world, we often miss it. Typically, people expect God to speak with an amplified voice or to talk to us through a burning bush, but God often speaks softly – like a whisper. We have to train our ears to hear His voice over all others. That's one of the fruits in the power of a disciplined life – hearing and knowing the voice of God. He won't always come rushing down at your every beck and call. He wants you to come up higher, where He is. Seeking Him ***will*** take some sacrifice. Find a peaceful place during a quiet point in your day to sit still and wait for the voice of the Lord to speak to you. In order to usher in His presence, you can begin by worshiping and praising God. Do this for as long as the Holy Spirit leads you. It is a good idea to have a notebook and pen with you to write down what He says.

The more you incorporate the practice of listening, the easier it will become. You will also find that just as you can train yourself to listen in the Spirit while it's quiet, you can also train your ears to hear Him in chaotic times and circumstances. This is so important because, as entrepreneurs, we can experience a lot of chaos on a daily basis. Yet, having the skill to find peace in the eye of the storm is such a blessing. Like all other skills, it will come with diligent practice. If you're experiencing silence from God, start expecting Him in unexpected places. It could be that He's given you an answer, but you keep asking for something other than what He's shown you. It may not be the right timing for an answer or you may need more maturity to comprehend the fullness of it. Silence can also mean that the answer requires patience and He wants you to seek Him more because there could be preliminary factors involved to get you to the desired end.

BOSS TRUTH #44

OWN YOUR PURPOSE

"For we are His workmanship, created in Christ Jesus for good works, which God prepared beforehand that we should walk in them."
–EPHESIANS 2:10

Be who you are, be comfortable in your skin, and walk boldly in your purpose. The Word of God says we are God's ***workmanship***. This means we were specially made and handcrafted by Him. Therefore, all those little things that make you who you are (even the imperfections) are pieces of the grand puzzle of what you're called to do. No one else has the qualities that God has put in you to accomplish your goals. ***They*** weren't made to tackle the challenges like a boss – ***you were!*** So who cares what people think?! You'd better own your purpose, and work it! This isn't just any purpose, it's ***your*** purpose, one that was prepared before you even knew your name.

My experience is that I always had the calling on my life to help entrepreneurs and ministries start or revamp their business, but I didn't want to because I felt this area wouldn't be profitable enough. I thought, "Is there a market for this?" When I began putting myself out there, the response I received was surprisingly positive. Other women approached me and said they weren't confident talking about God and business until they heard me speak. Now, on social media, many women in my circle are becoming bolder in this area and identifying God as part of their business. For this particular instance, I owned my confidence to boldly talk about my Creator and give Him credit for my entrepreneurial successes. What is it for you? Identify it and own it! As God's workmanship, there's so much that He's put in us, but we have to appreciate the value we have. Do this by taking chances and emphasizing the wonderful areas of yourself that you usually suppress ***for whatever reason***. You have to realize that someone needs what you already have!

BOSS TRUTH #45

BEWARE OF DREAM STEALERS

"Do not give what is holy to the dogs; nor cast your pearls before swine, lest they trample them under their feet, and turn and tear you in pieces."
–MATTHEW 7:6

You know that feeling when you come up with an amazing business idea, right? The first thing you want to do is share it with others so they can get excited about the idea too. But then, we encounter those – ***the haters*** – who ask: "Why would you want to do that? Did you go to school for that? You won't make any money doing that." At this point, you begin to second guess yourself and question what God has placed in your spirit. The "baby" God placed inside you begins to wither away and eventually dies because it wasn't strong enough to withstand the negativity. Just like a newborn baby, your dreams need to be protected. When you share your dreams prematurely, you risk aborting your destiny.

Jesus instructed us not to present what is sacred before fools (or the unwise). So I urge you to contain your excitement, and don't announce things before its time. Be silent until you are sure. And even when you are sure, never give away too much. Follow the Lord's lead here. He will reveal when the time is right.

BOSS TRUTH #46

OUTLINE YOUR LIFE

"For which of you, intending to build a tower, does not sit down first and count the cost, whether he has enough to finish it— "

–LUKE 14:28

I am a huge fan of outlining everything I do before I do it. I love to write things down. In fact, I have about 10 different notebooks for 10 different purposes. Outlined projects and ideas keep me organized. Writing is an amazing visual tool, and it's so simple to do. Whenever I have an idea, I write it down in my ***ideas book*** (yes, I actually have a book that says ideas on the cover, and I only use it for that purpose). I start by writing the date (super important), creating a headline (to remind myself later what the idea was about), and then I begin pouring my heart out. I sleep on it, and if I'm still excited about the idea in the morning, I ask the Holy Spirit to devise a plan of action: What do I need to do to get started today? Where do I need support from my team? When am I going to tell everyone about it?

When God gives you an idea, it doesn't necessarily have to come to fruition right away. Ideas are like seeds: we plant them and give them water and sunlight, and they bloom during their season. The key is to jot everything down and assess whether to act on the idea now or wait for the right season, ***or*** scrap it if it doesn't flow with your overall purpose. Just like Jesus gave the example of an intentional builder, are you counting the cost? Have you considered everything it's going to take to bring your dreams to fruition? Just as Jesus wants us to consider the cost of walking with Him, we are also to consider the cost of the resources associated with accomplishing our dreams. Outlining is the way to go. ***This makes for a successful business!*** Prove the God you serve by building something that lasts and endures for years to come.

BOSS TIP

Use the notes section to outline all the ideas and goals you have in your mind. Revisit your ideas daily to help you visualize your roadmap toward success.

NOTES

BOSS TRUTH #47

STAY FOCUSED

"Let your eyes look straight ahead, And your eyelids look right before you. Ponder the path of your feet, And let all your ways be established."
–PROVERBS 4:25-26

Distractions will come and the enemy will try to throw you curveballs to keep you unbalanced. This can be in the form of interruptions from people you love, provocations to constantly check social media for updates, unforeseen emergencies, etc. You will need to develop laser-like focus to accomplish your tasks. As a mother, expect your children to cry for you while you're on the phone with a client. As a wife, expect your husband to come to you with a major crisis (like "I can't find my shirt for work") when you're rushing out the door for a meeting...***classic***. Although you do have to make room for life to happen while you build your empire, you will need the discipline to get yourself back on track.

To stay focused and constantly keep your visions and goals in front of you, use sticky notes in your car, wallpapers on your phone, or dry erase markers on your mirror. I personally like to write out scriptures that describe the reason I work so hard and what my desired outcome is, such as Proverbs 13:22, ***"A good man leaves an inheritance to his children's children."*** It's also a good idea to have "go-to" people in times of distraction or stressful events. These are the people who will hold you accountable to what you said you would finish and who won't accept any excuses.

In trying times, it's so easy to think that what God said must have been our imagination, like: "Really God? I must have heard you wrong; surely you can't expect me to accomplish anything with the way my life looks right now." But God's response is still "Yes!" He knew every curveball that would ever be thrown your way, and yet He still trusts you to do great things. Think of how Zion cried out to the Lord in Isaiah 49:14, thinking He'd forgotten them. In the next verses He says, "Yet I will not forget you. See, I have inscribed you on the palms of ***My hands***; Your [city] walls ***are*** continually before Me."[26] Just remember that He has not forgotten you.

BOSS TRUTH #48

MAINTAIN MOMENTUM

"Do you not know that those who run in a race all run, but one receives the prize? Run in such a way that you may obtain it."
–1 CORINTHIANS 9:24

It's important to define what momentum is and what it isn't. It is the strength gained by a moving object. Momentum encompasses your personal goals, mindset, attitude, skills, network, and ability to take immediate action. Momentum is different from motion. ***Just because you're moving, doesn't mean you're gaining any valuable traction.*** When you start your journey, your momentum will likely be very high. There will be moments, however, when your momentum slows down or comes to a complete halt. This usually happens when:

a. You stop feeling challenged.
b. Difficulties feel impossible to overcome.
c. Money becomes more of a priority than joy.
d. You stop pushing for the best possible outcome and instead settle for mediocrity.

Just because your business slows down, doesn't mean you have to! Reflect back on the goals you set for yourself and your business in the previous chapters. Remind yourself of your passion and why you started your business. Approach every task with those goals in mind. Maintain your momentum by committing yourself to prayer and covering. Surround yourself with like-minded individuals who love and support you.

As believers, our ultimate prize is in Heaven, but that doesn't mean there aren't rewards established for us on earth as well. Keep running! Make your Father in Heaven proud and change some lives in the process!

BOSS TRUTH #49

REVISE AND REBUILD

"Let not your heart be troubled…"
–JOHN 14:1A

As you're listening in the Spirit, finding your focus, and maintaining momentum, you may find that there were steps you took in the past that you shouldn't have. Don't allow resentment to take over your thoughts. God not only builds; He restores. If you've made wrong decisions that didn't work out or overshot business moves that you were not prepared for, don't give up! Take time to process what could have been done better, revise your plan, tear down what didn't work, and start building again.

There is so much pressure to succeed in entrepreneurship, but don't let that pressure keep you from moving forward. Don't just "throw a rug on it" and keep going – troubleshoot issues now and you'll thank yourself later. Trust God in this process, and don't be too hard on yourself for having to start again. Just get it done the right way. He cares about quality, especially if you're a representation of Him!

BOSS TRUTH #50

SEEK WISE COUNSEL

"Without counsel, plans go awry, But in the multitude of counselors they are established."
–PROVERBS 15:22

Everybody, and their mother, will have an opinion about how you should run your business. And if you allow them, they will steer you toward confusion and failure. Even business-minded people who do not understand your unique calling can steer you down the wrong path. Your goal should be to seek wise counsel from individuals with renewed minds. The best way to find these individuals is to use discernment. Once you pray and ask God to reveal the right supporters for you, allow the Holy Spirit to confirm who is for you, and who isn't.

When I meet the people who God placed in my life to support me, I feel an unexplained pull toward them, and their words are invigorating when they speak. I still ask God for confirmation just to be confident. Your wise counselor will be knowledgeable, but more importantly, genuinely interested in you and your success. In the "multitude of counselors," you will gain insight into the areas that you are too close to see. When you find your support through counsel, cherish it, because you will receive in a minute what took them a year to learn.

BOSS CHALLENGE #5

Do you feel like you should be "friends" with everyone?

Are you concerned whether or not people will like you?

Have you compromised your calling to be a part of the crowd?

List five bold ways you will use to stand out among the crowd.

Put them into practice, and make a note of the results.

NOTES

CHAPTER 6

FEARLESS

BOSS TRUTH #51

DELIVER YOURSELF FROM PEOPLE

"The fear of man brings a snare,
But whoever trusts in the Lord
will be safe."
–PROVERBS 29:25

It's so easy to become distracted by the thoughts and opinions of others. Over the years, I literally had to train myself not to care what others thought of me. I remember when I began my entrepreneurial journey, people in my family would talk about me behind my back. They wondered what I was doing with my life, or whether I was doing anything at all. To be honest, it bothered me at first because I thought, "If they only knew how hard I was working, they wouldn't have anything negative to say." I worked hard to build what will become my legacy, and the fruits of my labour are present for everyone to witness.

The fear of man is a trap. It doesn't always mean you're literally fearful, but it can mean that you're looking to please people instead of being authentic to your purpose. If we base what we do on the reactions of those around us, we'll be stagnated our whole lives. James 1:6b-8 says, "For he who doubts is like a wave of the sea driven and tossed by the wind. For let not that man suppose that he will receive anything from the Lord; he is a double-minded man, unstable in all his ways." This describes exactly what the fear of man will do to you.

When you make the decision to become your own boss, you will have to develop an incredibly thick layer of tough skin because people will say things out of spite, pettiness, or sheer ignorance. I've been delivered from people since 1986 – when I left my mother's womb – and I don't have anyone to answer to except God. You don't have to care about anyone's opinion, except God's. He made you who you are and ***how*** you are. You got this far because of his grace and blessings, so who are they to tell you how you should live your life? Chile, bye! Let your confidence be rooted in the One who created you.

BOSS TRUTH #52

GET OUT OF YOUR OWN WAY

"Be steadfast, immovable, always abounding in the work of the Lord, knowing that your labor is not in vain in the Lord."
–1 CORINTHIANS 15:58

Sometimes, the only thing standing between you and greatness is you. Self-sabotage is a serious thing, and it's brought on by fear. While writing this book, I struggled to complete it. I kept thinking, "What if people don't like it? What if I put all this time and effort into it, and it doesn't sell?" I was halfway through writing my book, and I was ready to give up. Then, I remembered that fear is not of God! I had to think about who I really have to be accountable to, because if God told me to write this book, then I shouldn't allow the enemy to distract me from my goal. When you're on your way to creating something great, you will face the most opposition. That's how I know I am on the right path, and so I keep pushing.

I'm not one to quit, but quitting looks sweet when you're afraid of failure. I don't care whether you're afraid of fear, success, or losing friends. ***It doesn't matter***. Don't allow anything to come between you and success, including yourself! Attacks will try to throw you off course, but don't ever stand in your **own** way. Be firm and make the decision that you will not be moved from the course you've been set on.

BOSS TRUTH #53

LIVE BY POSSIBILITY

"For with God nothing will be impossible."
–LUKE 1:37

I want you to remove the word ***impossible*** from your vocabulary. Whatever we limit ourselves to in our minds stunts our growth. I've learned not to place limits on possibility because I serve a miracle-working God. I've also learned that if we don't remove the lid of possibility, we can never reach our truest potential. God's miracles don't just stop at their occurrence; they continue on to tell a story and to prove His greatness. ***He specializes in the unexpected.***

Luke 1 tells of the miraculous works and power of God. Just as Elizabeth was barren and thought she could not conceive, you might feel you can't bring your own "baby" to life. God is willing and able to accomplish miraculous things through you for His purpose and glory. Here are the steps you can take to begin living your life by possibility:

1. **Refuse to be average** - Remove *ordinary* and *status quo* from your life. Keep your foot on the gas, push forward, and continuously seek ways to innovate.
2. **Aim to be uncomfortable** - When you deliberately place yourself in uncomfortable situations, you will see growth. If you're too comfortable, you're not growing.
3. **Do something greater than yourself** - When we take on challenges that are bigger than ourselves, it requires us to trust God more and lean not on our own understanding. It also causes us to live in a place that inspires others to achieve greater possibilities.
4. **Understand that learning is a lifelong commitment** – When you get to a place where you think you know it all, you won't grow at all!

BOSS TRUTH #54

DON'T BE CONFINED BY OTHERS' PERCEPTION OF YOU

"...old things have passed away...all things have become new."
–2 CORINTHIANS 5:17B

Aggressive, opportunistic, failure...people love to use their own words to sum up who they ***think*** you are, especially those who don't know you. You may have been a teen mom and had people tell you that you wouldn't amount to anything. Yet, now you have the power to teach young girls about self-worth. You could have been a player in your young days, but now you teach young men that their bodies are temples and women are to be loved and not mistreated. ***Let me remind you of who God says you are:***

* ***You are a child of God.***[27]
* ***You are a branch of the true vine.***[28]
* ***You are a new creature in Christ.***[29]

Numerous times in the Bible, specific individuals had their names changed. This is significant because it represented a person coming into a new nature and a new season. Some of the most memorable name changes include: Abram to Abraham,[30] Sarai to Sarah,[31] Jacob to Israel[32] and Simon to Peter.[33] Abraham was becoming a father of a multitude. Sarah was becoming a mother of nations. Israel became powerful, and Peter was being called by Jesus to be the "rock"— a builder for the Kingdom of God. It's time to start asking God what ***your*** "new name" is. It doesn't matter who you were or what you did in the past. All that matters is ***who you are right now*** and all that you are destined to become. Don't be confined by what others think, but rather be defined by who God says you are.

BOSS TRUTH #55

RECOGNIZE YOUR SEASON

"To everything there is a season,
A time for every purpose
under heaven."
–ECCLESIASTES 3:1

Flowers don't bloom in the winter, just like trees don't shed their leaves in summer; there is a season for everything. The same is true for you and I. There are seasons when we plant seeds and earnestly await their growth. Then, there is a season when we reap all that we have sown. If you miss the seed-planting season, you won't have anything to reap come harvest time. Here are three ways to help you recognize your harvest season:

1. A shift in perspective - You begin to make a conscious decision to take a new approach to an old situation. A change happens, and your mind is renewed. You will begin to see your situation clearly, and feel confident walking in this new direction.

2. Confirmation - God always confirms things when we ask Him to. Personally, I always get a gut feeling when my situation is changing for the better, but I always ask for confirmation. Confirmation for me comes in the form of a prophetic word, or dream, but it could be different for you.

3. Abundance of opportunities - God allows good to come your way when you are ready to receive it. Not every opportunity is a ***God opportunity,*** but when you are in harvest season, you will find that all the right things start coming to you in a sequenced and methodical way. When opportunities come, you have to act immediately. There's no telling when or if the door of opportunity will ever open again.

Opportunities are like water to nurture each seed and help it grow. Dry seasons may come your way, and you will feel like nothing is happening. But keep praying for the rain to come. ***Rain only matters when you have seed in the ground.*** You may have a handful of crazy, ambitious ideas...***plant them all***. When the God opportunities come, seize them all and get ready to move to the next level!

BOSS TRUTH #56

JUMP AND A NET WILL APPEAR

"And Abraham called the name of the place, The-Lord-Will-Provide [Jehovah-Jireh]; as it is said to this day, In the Mount of the Lord it shall be provided."
–GENESIS 22:14

If you don't step out on faith and put yourself out there, you can never truly take advantage of all the Lord has for you. You may be scared of uncertainties and so you procrastinate, but ***fear does not come from God***. Procrastination is a physical manifestation of fear. The Lord God is our provider, and He has promised to supply all of our needs – we just have to keep the right perspective. It's natural to be concerned, so let's examine the what-ifs:

* What if I fail? vs What if I win?!
* What if I'm not good enough? vs What if I turn out to be the best?
* What if I'm not ready? vs What if I'm actually prepared?

I'm not suggesting you jump before the time is right; just don't allow fear to be the reason you don't jump at all. No matter which what-if applies to you, God has your answer and provision. Indecision and inactivity leave you stuck in the middle! Don't be the hold-up for your own success. Here's some advice to help you tread unfamiliar waters:

1. Calculate your risks. Are you ready to jump? Assess how high you arwilling to jump before you do. This can include factors such as relocation, and levels of commitment.

2. Pray for supernatural faith. If you're lacking in this department, it will be difficult for you to leap into the unknown.

3. Remember the Holy Spirit is with you every step of the way. As much as it may seem like you're doing this alone, the Lord is with you ***always***.

BOSS TRUTH #57

STEP OUTSIDE YOUR COMFORT ZONE

"God has not given us a spirit of fear, but of power and of love and of a sound mind."
–2 TIMOTHY 1:7

You can never truly be extraordinary if you refuse to step outside your comfort zone. You have to look at fear as an intruder. It steals your hope, your dreams, and your future. God says fear is ***not*** supposed to rule us! Even the most successful people experience fear, but the difference is ***they don't let it control their lives***. If God says we've been given power instead of fear, then it's up to us to trust our power when we encounter fear. Here are some real-life examples:

* If there's a potential opportunity but a response from the other party has been delayed, ***you*** pursue them until you get what you require.
* Don't be creepy, but if you know you want to connect with someone extraordinary and you know their social hangout spot, stop in the area and introduce yourself.
* When buying, selling, or negotiating a deal, have faith and ask for what you want instead of settling for what people will give you.

Take a stand for your future and go out and get what God says you can have. Forget about being rational, because sometimes rules are just limitations. I'm not saying you have to be cutthroat, but if there's something God has led you to, step outside your comfort zone and go get it!

BOSS TRUTH #58

BE ANXIOUS FOR NOTHING

*"Be anxious for nothing,
but in everything by prayer and
supplication, with thanksgiving,
let your requests be made
known to God."*
–PHILIPPIANS 4:6

Anxiety is a manifestation of indecision and doubt; the overwhelming frustration of the unknown. Imagine driving in an unfamiliar place and your Google Maps stops working. You have no reception. Then, your phone dies...***and*** you have no portable charger (story of my life). The emotions felt at that moment can manifest into anxiety. I'm sure we all know what it's like to have a goal set in our minds only to be met by a curveball that shifts everything out of our control. God is still in control even when we get stuck and don't know how ***or where*** to go. The same is true in business. When we lose our "GPS signal," we lose our sense of direction, but we have to revert back to God for instruction.

The antidote for anxiety is prayer. You will have to recalibrate your spirit and find God's instruction and provision for you ***in that moment***. Matthew 6:34 says, "Do not worry about tomorrow, for tomorrow will worry about its own things. Sufficient for the day is its own trouble."

Overcome anxiety by engaging yourself in prayer one day at a time, and you will see God's will and great peace unfold in your life and business. When we make our requests known to God, we remove all sense of anxiety because we know that ***He knows*** what's best for us. Continually thank God in the good times ***and*** the bad, and watch how He keeps you.

BOSS TIP

What are some of the things you're anxious about? Write them down in your *Boss Journal*, and use them as a guide in prayer. Call out each of those anxieties and ask the Holy Spirit to bring you a sense of peace concerning them.

BOSS TRUTH #59

NO GUTS NO GLORY

—

"Be strong and of good courage, do not fear nor be afraid of them; for the Lord your God, He is the One who goes with you. He will not leave you nor forsake you."
–DEUTERONOMY 31:6

Deuteronomy 31:6 displays the reassurance that the Israelites had as Joshua was taking over leadership from Moses. They were headed into a new land (that was surprisingly occupied already). God's promise was that He would be with them and that they would go and possess ***all*** He had for them. They weren't supposed to wait for the land to be delivered into their hands. They were supposed to rise up and take back what was theirs to begin with. This approach was completely new to them. The Israelites were so used to Moses' leadership, wandering through the wilderness, and being fed daily from the sky by God. But now, Joshua's wisdom[34] was about to be poured out, and they were finally reaching the promised land. Cultivation of this land and the defeat of their enemies was inevitable.

The baton was being passed on to Joshua and the stewardship and judgments of an entire nation were now in his hands...***now that takes guts!*** Right now, the baton is being passed on to you and you are going to heights you've never experienced. Remember, exceptional results do not happen within standard parameters. Break free from the norm! It takes courage to stand in the face of adversity, to lead others, and to do something impactful. Do you want to be number one? Move through the fear to see and realize your true self. Your glory waits on the other side.

BOSS TRUTH #60

BE A GO-GETTER

"In all labor there is profit,
But idle chatter leads only to poverty."
–PROVERBS 14:23

As a child of God, you were born to succeed. Period. Be willing to do whatever it takes to move ahead. Be willing to explore the greatness inside you. Dedicate as much time as it takes to achieve your goals – it could take weeks, months, or years. Don't accept defeat as an option – ***dust yourself off and try again***. You can only talk about a dream so much before it becomes stagnant. Now is the time to get up and start moving. Wipe the dust off those plans that have been pushed to the back burner. Reconnect with your network, continue your research, and seek opportunities for advancement.

You have to be willing to take risks and leap into the unknown. You must be willing to trust God with your life, and accept that you cannot do it on your own. Only the hungry survive in the world of entrepreneurship...only those willing to do whatever it takes – ***ethically of course*** – to achieve greatness will succeed. Don't just talk about it, ***be*** about it.

BOSS CHALLENGE #6

Are you allowing fear to prevent you from receiving all God has for you? Join the five-day Zero Fear challenge. Go to www.tamarhuggins.com/bossedup to join the challenge! Over the course of five days, you will take the necessary steps to eliminate fear from your life.

CHAPTER 7

LEADERSHIP

BOSS TRUTH #61

WHEN THERE IS NO VISION, PEOPLE PERISH

"Where there is no revelation [prophetic vision], the people cast off restraint..."
–PROVERBS 29:18A

The Israelites constantly fell into apostasy whenever their current leader passed away. Due to their cycles of disobedience, God allowed their enemies to conquer them. Once they repented, a deliverer was sent to remind them of God's plan and lead them out of captivity to triumph over their enemies. One instance of this is in Judges 4. Under the strong leadership of Deborah, the only female judge in the Bible, the Israelites were delivered out of oppression in Canaan and into victory. An important lesson in leadership is that people ***need*** to be led, whether they know it or not. God is the ultimate leader, who always provides His people with a plan. Throughout history, His design is to appoint leaders as governors over His specific plans and strategies to overcome obstacles.[35] Without a constant reminder of the vision, people lose faith and direction.

I want you to keep this principle in mind as you lead in your business. It is God's vision for humanity to move toward righteousness and be redeemed back to Him. Think about where your business and dreams are going. Your vision is your roadmap. If you don't produce, verbalize, and implement your vision for your team or yourself, you cannot expect things to go in the direction you intended. Whatever you have to do, keep it clear and comprehensible. Also, keep the vision physically visible. Whether it's in your email signature or hanging on the walls of your office, make your vision attractive and motivational so that those working with you are reminded ***why*** they are there and ***what*** they're working toward.

BOSS TRUTH #62

LEAD WITH INTEGRITY

"Providing honorable things, not only in the sight of the Lord, but also in the sight of men."
–2 CORINTHIANS 8:21

Integrity is an important value of mine because it encompasses honesty, credibility, and sincerity – all the qualities I strive to maintain as a child of God. These qualities are all necessary for successful leadership, and it takes ***time*** to build and ***effort*** to maintain them. As a leader, these qualities manifest in the way you speak and respond to your emotions and the emotions of others around you.

It isn't enough to display integrity in your work environment alone. ***It has to be who you really are, even behind closed doors.*** If you feel like you struggle with integrity, the first step is admitting it to yourself and to God. Repent and allow God to work on your values and ethics, because integrity ***cannot*** be faked. Maintaining integrity is as simple as paying people on time, owning your mistakes, and remaining true to your word. If you say you are going to do something, ***do it***. If you make a mistake, no matter how embarrassing, ***own it***. Your goal as a leader is to build trust and maintain the loyalty of those you lead.

BOSS TRUTH #63

LEADERS NEED LEADERS

—

"A wise man will hear
and increase learning,
And a man of understanding will
attain wise counsel."
–PROVERBS 1:5

You don't know it all. I repeat, ***you do not know it all!*** There comes a time when you have to own your weaknesses and then select the right people to fill in the gaps. I am a huge supporter of mentorship. I believe that every business leader needs to be mentored by someone who is willing to share their knowledge and coach you toward becoming a better leader. Here are some tips on receiving mentorship:

1. **Do the work:** Please don't approach anyone, especially someone of a higher stature, if you haven't done any work. In-depth research needs to be complete, books need to be read, courses need to be taken, etc. You want to show your potential mentor that you are ready and capable of being mentored. No one wants to waste their time on someone who doesn't help themselves first, ***before*** seeking support.
2. **Don't ask to pick anyone's brain:** It's a proven fact that most people don't value what they get for free. It's insulting to ask a professional for free information if they make their living by providing that same information to others. Please understand that you will need to invest money in certain types of resources.
3. **Implement suggestions:** There is nothing more annoying than having someone ask for help, and when provided, they do nothing to progress. One important way to show your mentor that you value their expertise is to implement what they suggest.
4. **Offer something of value:** Many people believe that a mentor/mentee relationship is one-sided, when in fact it is give-and-take. It takes a lot of energy to mentor someone, and it can be very draining spiritually. I want you to enter into your mentorship with a "How can I help my mentor?" attitude vs "How can they help me?" Pouring back into your mentor can be as simple as sending them an encouraging word or praying for their strength. The simple things count.

BOSS TRUTH #64

YOU HAVE TO BUILD IN ORDER TO MAINTAIN

"Moreover you shall select from all the people able men…"
–EXODUS 18:21A

A great example of effective leadership is seen in the life of Moses. Moses' task of finding solutions for the people of Israel was way beyond his capabilities. It was his wise father-in-law who warned him of burnout if he carried out his tasks without engaging others to help him. Exodus 18:21-23 in the Message Bible says:

"Keep a sharp eye out for competent men-men who fear God, men of integrity, men who are incorruptible-and appoint them as leaders over groups organized by the thousand, by the hundred, by fifty, and by ten. They'll be responsible for the everyday work of judging among the people. They'll bring the hard cases to you, but in the routine cases they'll be the judges. They will share your load and that will make it easier for you. If you handle the work this way, you'll have the strength to carry out whatever God commands you, and the people in their settings will flourish also."

This proves how recognizing the gifts, skills, and talents in your team are essential to your own accomplishments. Stop believing you are meant to work alone. We are all standing on the shoulders of other people. Pretending we can handle it all often leads to burnout and discouragement.

Moses also learned the importance of building strategic alliances. Strategic alliances can be described as a coming together of two or more parties who agree to certain behaviours or procedures for the purpose of ultimately creating mutually beneficial results. I challenge you to build your own strategic alliances. Any form of relationship building requires genuine commitment if it is to work. Pray that God gives you the energy required to build as many strategic alliances as possible. Be patient, and remember that relationships take time to yield results.

BOSS TRUTH #65

TRUE LEADERS ARE ANOINTED AND APPOINTED

"The Lord makes poor and makes rich; He brings low and lifts up."
–1 SAMUEL 2:7

As a boss, you are a natural leader. God has already called you forth and given you the aptitude to function in a leadership capacity. At some point, you will raise up other leaders to help you run your business. If you're like me, you will start your business as a sole entity and run it by yourself for a while before your team is built. This is normal. When the first person comes along, it will be tempting to hand over the bulk of the load you have carried on your own for so long. However, I caution you, choose your leaders wisely.

Promotion comes from the Lord, not man. In 1 Samuel, we learn about the appointment of Saul by the people of Israel as king over the nation. Saul displayed the outward appearance of a king, but the truth is, he was insufficient.[38] Insufficient leaders make costly mistakes. Instead, what Israel needed was David, a man after God's heart. He didn't stand seven feet tall like Saul did, nor did he display any of the typical appearances of a king. Yet, he became the most notable king in the world because of his heart. ***The popular choice isn't always the best choice***, and the scriptures show us how those rejected by men have often been chosen by God.

Your business is your baby, and it is precious. If you want to be successful, you can't have anyone other than those anointed and appointed by God working in your business. You know your business well, and God knows you. The best way to build your team is to:

*Understand the purpose of your business and the areas where you need the most support.

*Increase your own leadership acumen by reading and studying books on leadership.

*Pray for the right individuals to come and fulfill their role. Be specific in your prayer so that you can identify who God has sent to support your business.

BOSS TIP

Use your *Boss Journal* to describe your ideal partner or employee. List all the qualities and skills you would like them to have. Pray on it, and ask God to confirm that what you want is actually what you need. If you have no idea what you need, ask God to reveal the gaps where you'll need support in the future. Write down what He shows you, and keep an eye out for the people He will send to help you.

NOTES

BOSS TRUTH #66

LET FAITH LEAD YOU

"Now faith is the substance of things hoped for, the evidence of things not seen."
–HEBREWS 11:1

Are you ***faithful*** or ***faithless***? I can't stress how important having faith is to your success as an entrepreneur. Through this process, you will be tested a lot, and the strength of your faith will determine how far you go. Many people say they have faith, but as soon as the challenges come, their faith fails. Abraham is an excellent model of faith in the Bible. He walked with God and was faithful and obedient. He had faith when God told him to leave his home in Chaldea to travel to Canaan.[39] He also believed God for the land and the promise that his seed would be like the stars of Heaven.[40]

God led Abraham into places he didn't know, and God will do the same for you. He will give you the territory you desire and the inheritance, as long as you have faith. Are you walking in faith, or are you working through your flesh? The Word of God says that the flesh goes against the Spirit and vice versa. It is antagonistic to the workings of the Holy Spirit and causes people to oppose the bold and good things that God intended.[41] Accordingly, you are not to put trust in man – including yourself! Put your trust in God alone, for He shall direct your path. Pray for the faith of Abraham. Ask God to show you how to trust him. Then, let go and allow Him to lead you.

BOSS TRUTH #67

PAY YOUR DUES

"...If anyone will not work, neither shall he eat."
–2 THESSALONIANS 3:10

You are never done paying your dues, and neither am I. The moment you think you are, you've set yourself up for failure. Paying your dues is about earning respect by working hard, gaining valuable experience, and retaining integrity. The Word says that we are to be like the ant when it comes to work.[42] They have no overseer or ruler, yet they prepare extensively for harvest season. So, if insects instinctively work hard, why should we think any different about ourselves?

God-given power is never placed into unqualified hands. Your goal is to earn comfort in knowing that, at the end of it all, you have given your absolute best and the Lord is pleased. When you're not building and doing your part, you're considered a sluggard and comparable to someone who does not build but tears down.[43] If you're not ***adding to,*** then you're ***taking away*** or ***hindering progress***. Just as the "early bird gets the worm," it is the "hardworking farmer who gets the first of the harvest."[44]

BOSS TRUTH #68

TEACH THE NEXT GENERATION

"Now also when I am old and grayheaded, O God, do not forsake me, Until I declare Your strength to this generation, Your power to everyone who is to come."
–PSALM 71:18

King David had such a strong desire to do the will of God and to complete His work before he left the earth. And in spite of those who plotted against and sought his life, his plea before God in his old age was that he would get to instill the works and ways of God into those coming up after him. His exhortation before God, in Psalm 71, is a great example of what our demeanor should be. It should be one of urgency and not obligation. In other words, "We ***get*** to teach the next generation," not "We ***have*** to teach the next generation." Consider it a privilege and an opportunity that God would use you to pass on wisdom and experience.

What good is it for us to gain knowledge, wisdom, and understanding and keep it to ourselves? As mentioned before, I am a firm believer in mentorship; it is such an important element to the success of future generations. Once upon a time, someone gave you advice, support, or encouragement that helped you make the leap into entrepreneurship. So pass it on – ***be a hero and mentor someone.*** Help them become the person God intended them to be. A wise friend of mine once said, "A victory is not a true victory unless it's shared." She's right! Make the moments of your life matter by inviting people to share in your victory. Teach them how you overcame. No one ever said mentors had to be perfect; it's transparency and effectiveness that counts.

Also, mentorship doesn't have to take a lot of time. There are ways to make it work. For example, if your schedule tends to be tight from week to week, a mentee can simply ride along with you during errands or lunch breaks. Or, if it's someone you've been mentoring for a while and a level of trust has been established, perhaps they can sit in on meetings or accompany you when you travel abroad. Conversely, if your schedule is more open, take advantage of that and set aside quality sit-down time with your mentee(s). Either way, it's good to incorporate "field time" ***and*** "quality time," but your schedule can determine which one you engage in the most.

In addition to schedule considerations, let your mentee determine the depth of each meeting or session. Understand where they are and meet them there, but also challenge them. It can be an encouraging word or piece of advice to change someone's life for the better. It can even be as extensive as helping them progress through life's tough decisions. However simple or complex, it should always be consistent and intentional, until the desired goal or end has been achieved. Just as the Lord used others and poured into you, you shall pour into another.

BOSS TIP

Mentor one person for every two people who helped you.

NOTES

BOSS TRUTH #69

GO ONWARD AND UPWARD

"As iron sharpens iron,
so a man sharpens the
countenance of his friend."
–PROVERBS 27:17

I'm sure you've heard the saying, "You can't take everyone with you." I'm sure you've also heard stories of successful people "changing" or "forgetting where they came from." No matter what side you view it from, the fact still remains that your circle shifts as you go higher in life. I just shared the importance of being mentored and mentoring someone who is up and coming. Now, I want you to understand how important it is to mentor ***your own*** team.

When you reach a new level of success, your needs change and you will require more output from the people around you. It is your responsibility as a leader to recognize the calling in each of your team members and to support them in areas they are lacking so they can support you in new ways. For example, you may have a person on your team whose skill level in a particular area is about a seven out of ten, but at your new level of growth, you require someone with skills that are a nine out of ten. I've been in this position a few times before, and I made it up in my mind that I would not drop the person who was with me from the beginning. Instead, I had an open conversation about what my needs were and what I was willing to do to help them.

For you, it could mean paying for a mini part-time course so they can sharpen their skills, or connecting them to a mentor who is more senior in their field. As long as they are willing to learn (and they should be), I want you to do everything you can to sharpen them. ***That's love.*** When people recognize their own value, they will increase it. Your company's most valuable resource is its human capital. So surround yourself with people you can support and – most importantly – who can support you.

BOSS TRUTH #70

CREATE A LEGACY WORTH REMEMBERING

"A good man leaves an inheritance to his children's children…"
–PROVERBS 13:22A

It is your duty to your children to leave a legacy for them. A legacy can be defined as something valuable that is left behind through a relative or a leader. People can either be born into a legacy or acquire its benefits through favourable positioning and opportunity. God lives within you, and as such, you are destined for greatness. You have the right to live a life that is fulfilled and vibrant with extraordinary experiences. You should live in such a way that the impact of your life remains long after you're gone. This has nothing to do with status or widespread popularity, but with the quality and richness of the things you produce, build, and sustain.

Everything I do creates impact, whether it's in my industry or on the lives of those around me. And I do that ***on purpose***. Even though I operate different businesses and work in different environments, the same goal is driving me: ***to know that when I leave this earth, the work I did continues to inspire others to do better and to be better.*** I exist for a reason, and so do you! Identify what mark you want to leave. What will people say about you after you're gone? Even better, what will God have to say about the impressions you left? No matter what has been done, your footprint still matters! Don't allow intimidation or anything else to hold you back. In a world full of "copy and pasters," dare to do something new. Recognize your power. Own your purpose, and make it your life. Find your place and leave your undeniable mark! When you do, you'll have a legacy worth remembering.

BOSS CHALLENGE #7

If you don't have a mentor, I encourage you to reach out to someone who is excelling in your field and ask them whether they are willing to mentor you. Some mentors do charge a fee, while others may do it at no cost to you. Once you have gained adequate knowledge through mentorship and education, find a mentee and share that knowledge with him or her. Use the space here to make notes on information learned or shared through your mentorship.

NOTES

CHAPTER 8

PERSEVERANCE

BOSS TRUTH #71

YOU ARE UNLIKE ANY OTHER

—

"...And not one of them [sparrows] falls to the ground apart from your Father's will. But the very hairs of your head are all numbered. Do not fear therefore; you are of more value than many sparrows."
–MATTHEW 10:29B-31

God created you unlike anyone else. From the number of hairs on your head to the way you walk and think, there are no mistakes. ***You*** are not a mistake. You are an important part of God's master plan, so take honor and pride in that. You came into this world with a very specific plan, strengths, and abilities. Keep in mind that the Lord never gives us more than we can bear. So if you've gone through really hard times, congratulations! All that means is that you were designed with the strength to overcome it. You are literally tougher than you think. If God gave your burdens to another, they might not be able to handle it. Why? They weren't built like you.

Trials not only come to make us stronger, but also to reveal hidden qualities that set us apart. Two people can go through the exact same situation, but triumph in two completely different ways. ***How*** you overcome matters just as much as the overcoming itself. For me, I've found that perseverance is a strong and natural quality of mine. It's just not in my DNA to quit or back down from a challenge. Even when things look bleak, I tap into the reserve of strength God built within me, and I keep pushing. For you, it could be your joy or faith that got you through challenging times. Perhaps it was your preparation before the "storm" even hit, or it could have been your ability to bounce back quickly. However your victory comes, take note of it because it says something significant about what God has placed within you.

Challenges can be a humbling experience. Think of Jesus. The ***only*** way He was going to accomplish His great assignment was with humility. That was His key! In the Garden of Gethsemane, He asked God whether that "cup" could be taken from Him, but it was the will of the Father that He continue on His journey. Philippians 2:8 says, "And being found in appearance as a man, He humbled Himself and became obedient to the point of death at the cross." There are various characteristics God placed in you that only storms can ignite. Don't be so quick to be delivered from the pressures you're facing, but rather ask God to reveal the keys He's given you to master the challenge. Your success as an entrepreneur is not only based on how hard you work and how knowledgeable you become, but how strategically you navigate using the advantageous gifts God has given you. Moreover, these gifts shine the brightest under pressure ***if*** you're willing and yielding. Just remember that if not one bird falls from the air without the Father knowing about it, then surely He has not forgotten about you!

NOTES

BOSS TRUTH #72

FAIL FAST

"Trust in the Lord with all your heart, And lean not on your own understanding. In your ways acknowledge Him, And He shall direct your paths."
–PROVERBS 3:5-6

I want you to ignore everything you've ever understood failure to be, because one of the most powerful catalysts for success is failure. The faster you fail, the closer you are to the solution. I know it sounds tough in the moment, but believe me when I tell you it's true. When you're down, don't stay down. The best thing to do after a failure is to quickly get up, analyze what went wrong, and move forward. Don't let failures bring a halt to your momentum. ***Everyone*** messes up from time to time, but the quicker you shake off the disappointment, the quicker you can get back on track.

Keep in mind that the bigger the goal, the higher the risk of failure. It's all about setting rational expectations. When I started my nonprofit, I was dead set on who I wanted to reach. I knew I wanted to support and strengthen tech startups led by minority entrepreneurs, but I didn't realize how difficult it would be. For each application round, I didn't see as many women or people of colour as I would have liked to see, and I couldn't understand why. Although my nonprofit helped our resident startups raise over $1.1 million in capital, I still felt like something was missing. Other companies had much higher enrollment rates than I did, and I couldn't understand why (because, truthfully, our entrepreneurship program was much stronger). Then, it hit me!

I realized that I had been going about it all wrong. If I wanted to see more diversity in tech, I had to pivot my existing model and focus on educating our youth. If our youth didn't believe that technology was a viable option for them, they would never pursue it as a career and I would never create the impact I wanted. So, basically, my mistake was making the false assumption that there were ***already enough*** women and people of colour that I could train and support. I failed fast enough and was able to shift my strategy and continue in the right direction.

If you don't experience failure, you're not pushing hard enough. Your goal shouldn't be to avoid failure, but rather to use Godly wisdom in the face of it. This is why we can't lean on our own understanding. Sometimes, we can be so headstrong thinking we have it all figured out that we don't stop to inquire about the things we could be missing. ***The small details matter***, and can bring clarity as well as lighten the load of our struggle.

Do you ever wonder ***why*** "all things work together for good to those who love God"?[45] It's because God is infinite and all-powerful! There is nothing He can't recover or transform. Whether circumstances were your fault or that of another, He is ***still*** able to reconcile what you lost. So if you're failing, ***fail fast***, because your victory is right around the corner!

NOTES

BOSS TRUTH #73

DON'T DESPISE SMALL BEGINNINGS

"For who has despised the day of small things?"
–ZECHARIAH 4:10

I am a very ambitious woman. I love to set high expectations for myself, and I love a good challenge. One of the mistakes I made over the years was disregarding the significance of my smaller accomplishments. It wasn't that I didn't care about them, I just never took the time to notice their importance to the greater good. Then, a friend helped me understand the importance of slowing down and celebrating the small wins. Why? They lead to greater victories, and without them, I wouldn't accomplish major goals or appreciate how far I've come.

We all work so hard to make our dreams a reality, and we deserve to acknowledge ourselves for a job well done. If you don't take notice of the smaller accomplishments, you may begin to feel like you aren't getting anywhere. The truth is, everything you do now is a stepping stone to something much greater. A good way to acknowledge your small wins is to log them. Write your accomplishments in your ***Boss Journal***. Each week or month (depending on how fast-paced your business is), be determined to write down what your business achieved or what you accomplished – no matter how great or how insignificant it may seem in the moment. Doing this not only helps you track your progress, but it creates a culture of gratefulness within your life and business.

BOSS TRUTH #74

GET HEALED FROM EMOTIONAL HURTS

"He heals the brokenhearted and binds up their wounds."
–PSALM 147:3

Before you put yourself out there with your exciting new ideas and business concepts, I want you to conduct an internal scan. No, not at the doctor's office, because no doctor knows you that well. Instead, ask Jehovah Rapha – God, our healer – to make known any and all emotional hurts you might be suffering from. It could be feelings of rejection, or perhaps you never received words of affirmation as a child and it left a scar. Just know that God heals, restores, and makes us whole, but the first step is ***realizing*** that you need inner healing.

Emotional healing is important because, if left unaddressed, those same hurts will resurface in your business. For example, when it's time for you to promote your business, you become fearful of hearing the word "No" so you avoid asking customers to buy your product. Or, due to a lack of confidence, you may never feel comfortable putting your services or products out there because you feel you aren't good enough. These are lies from the pits of hell! God knows your heart, He sees your pain, and He wants to heal you, but you must allow Him to.

Emotional healing can begin with intensifying your prayer time with God. It is a good idea to have wise people around who will support you during your healing process. Once you ask God to surface the things in your heart that could hold you back, it might seem like your life is flipping upside down. ***Don't panic.*** This is a completely normal part of the process. It's like having to mend a broken bone that healed the wrong way. Some things in your life might feel like they're breaking all over again, but God's purpose is to help you heal the right way. The healing process will secure your future, safeguard your heart, and make the vision He's put in you unbreakable.

You will know that healing is taking place when you no longer react the same way to situations that once triggered negative emotions. You will not only see it in your actions, but in your thoughts as well. When a negative word is uttered, old memories will not resurface. You won't take certain things personally. Instead, you will begin to see your situation from God's perspective. Then, you'll be on your way to becoming the impactful entrepreneur God intended you to be.

BOSS TRUTH #75

LET JESUS TAKE THE WHEEL

"Cast your burden on the Lord,
And He shall sustain you;
He shall never permit
the righteous to be moved."
–PSALM 55:22

"J***esus take the wheel"*** is a popular saying, and there is so much importance in that phrase. Jesus gives us His shoulders to carry the burden. If He has already "borne our griefs and carried our sorrows,"[46] then there's not much else left for us to do but trust Him. You might not realize this, but worrying is almost as bad as sin because it shows a lack of trust, which can lead to carnal actions to deliver ***ourselves*** out of problems. He alone is the one who offers us rest, so:

* In those moments when you want to give up, let ***Jesus take the wheel.***
* When you feel you aren't good enough, let ***Jesus take the wheel.***
* When a business deal falls through, let ***Jesus take the wheel.***
* When your partner gives up on the business, let ***Jesus take the wheel.***
* When you're broke and need a breakthrough, let ***Jesus take the wheel.***

Our stance in God comes from our faith in believing He won't allow us to be moved. This means that He's holding on to us and ***never*** letting go, but on our end, separation from God is a choice. When we realize that God is not as emotional as we are, maybe we'll stop being so fickle with Him. Persevere knowing that ***absolutely nothing*** can separate you from ***His*** love.[47]

BOSS TRUTH #76

BAD DECISIONS MAKE GREAT TESTIMONIES

"Come and hear, all you who fear God, And I will declare what He has done for my soul."
–PSALM 66:16

Bad decisions...we've all made them, from hiring the wrong person for an important position to mismanaging money. The fact is we're human, and making mistakes is natural. What's important is that you ***learn*** from your mistakes, instead of repeating them. Chances are, if you are aiming to do something great, you will make some bad decisions along the way. So, just how it is with your soul when you were redeemed, your business can go through times of redemption where God's hand reaches in to save it. And just how we testify of His goodness toward us spiritually, we should testify of His goodness in our business when ***we know*** we've messed up!

As you're shooting for higher ground, the wisdom you gain from making bad decisions should most definitely outweigh the consequences (even though the consequences can be tough to deal with). The number of times you fall is not comparable to the awesome fact that you can rise up again. The Word says that the righteous are not exempt from challenging experiences, but we do have a ***good shepherd*** walking right beside us every step of the way. Have joy in your process; don't be afraid to look back and laugh at things you could have done better. The stress of condemnation alone is enough to drive a person crazy. In fact, think of all the people you're going to help by preventing them from going down that same road. Focus your thinking on the fact that it is a blessing to ***be*** a blessing.

BOSS TRUTH #77

LEARN TO ENCOURAGE YOURSELF

*"These things I have spoken to you,
that in Me you may have peace.
In the world you will have tribulation;
but be of good cheer, I have
overcome the world."*
–JOHN 16:33

You have high aspirations. As a result, those who don't will try to pull you down. Some people want to see you doing well, but not better than them. It's an unfortunate truth, but don't worry about them (they need Jesus!). Instead, reflect on the words of encouragement from the Lord. He has already overcome every situation you will ever face. It is perfectly healthy and normal to want to hear the words: "Good Job! Keep going! You can do it!" However, to ***depend*** on them is unrealistic. Don't get me wrong; I get it. You work so hard and do so much that at the end of the day, it would be a breath of fresh air for someone – ***anyone*** – to say a word of praise. The reality is that you won't always get that luxury. You may not always run into that person who lifts your spirits during the bad days, so you have to learn how to give kudos to yourself.

Self-encouragement is a discipline, and you have to train yourself to think beyond your current challenge. It's understandable at the beginning of your journey to be flooded with so much hope and confirmation, but there comes a time when God expects us to mature and to trust Him. You can't build your dreams on the backs of other people's faith. At some point, you have to ***know*** that you will make it ***because God said you would!***

BOSS TIP

I am a big believer in words of affirmation, and I want to share mine with you. Visit www.tamarhuggins.com/bossedup to view my personal 31 Daily Affirmations. Be inspired. Learn to encourage yourself to keep going.

BOSS TRUTH #78

RELEASE FAMILY AND FRIENDS FROM SUPPORT BONDAGE

"...From whence comes my help? My help comes from the Lord."
–PSALM 121:1B-2A

What is support bondage? It's when we, as entrepreneurs, apply pressure on our family and friends to support our business. And if they don't support us, we lay the guilt trip on them. How many of you are going to be honest and admit that you've placed your family and friends into support bondage? It's natural for us to look to our friends and family to support our business. We expect them to buy our products and use our services, right? Well guess what...your friends and family are not your target market! They may not feel like supporting you because they cannot identify with what you have to offer, ***and that's OK.***

Why are you limiting your client base to your circle of friends and family anyway? Instead, you need to pray that God enlarges your coast, so that you can reach the people who are searching for the solution your business provides. Family may be good for practice and just getting your feet off the ground, but they should not be your only customers. It's time to graduate from that mindset so those who ***need*** your product or service can receive and benefit from it. Trust me, you'll want to save yourself the frustration anyway, because sometimes blood is the only thing that ties families together. You can want so badly for your friends and family to share your interests and passions, but it doesn't always happen that way and you have to accept that reality. One thing I ***have*** found is that even though my family isn't involved in everything I do, they're great advertisers! In conversation, they're quick to say: "Hey! My daughter can help with that!" or "My sister works with people like this; you should give her a call." So just take a moment, take a breath, and free them. It's not the end of the world. If they're on board, great. If not, that's OK, too.

BOSS TIP

One way your family and friends can support you is through word of mouth promotion. Even if *they* aren't in the market for your product or service, they may know someone who is!

NOTES

BOSS TRUTH #79

ONLY THE PERSISTENT REAP BENEFITS

"And let us not grow weary while doing good, for in due season we shall reap if we do not lose heart."
–GALATIANS 6:9

The one thing worse than failure is losing hope. Sometimes, it's easy to think that if our "due season" isn't coming fast enough, it must not be coming at all. ***Don't give in to these thoughts.*** You will lose many things in your lifetime, but if you lose hope, it's very difficult to get it back. Romans 12:12 tells us to "***rejoice*** in hope, be patient in tribulation, and remain in constant prayer." Let worship anchor you, and remember that no matter how stagnant you might feel, God is always working for you behind the scenes. He renews our strength. He mounts us up like the wings of an eagle! You've got to keep going, because you never know how close you are to your breakthrough. Keep the promises of God at the forefront of your mind, but don't get so caught up in the future that you don't maintain the present.

What God is doing in you now is just as important as what He's going to do in the future. For example, I've been through seasons where it seemed like I had all the answers for everyone except myself. ***Each time,*** they received exactly what they needed from God ***through me!*** They received revelations, resources, answers, connections, and so much more. Then, when it seemed like I was close to my breakthrough, it ended in roadblocks. I said, "God, are you serious?! You mean to tell me that you're using me to be everyone else's answer while I still don't have my own?!" I soon came to understand that He was teaching me about perseverance and selflessness. That season was a tough one, yet I found joy in what God was doing in the lives of others around me. And even though it was a bittersweet season, I wouldn't trade it for anything in the world. I saw His hand move in so many miraculous ways, and I learned that whether I'm the vessel or the receiver, God is still good.[48]

BOSS TRUTH #80

SACRIFICES HAVE TO BE MADE

"But you, be strong and do not let your hands be weak, for your work shall be rewarded!"

–2 CHRONICLES 15:7

Close to the end of my maternity leave, I remember calling my boss and asking him whether he would allow me to work from home. I thought that if I could stay at home, I could manage my time between my one-year-old daughter and my new business. He understood my position, but told me it wouldn't be possible because working from home was not part of their policy. At that moment, I decided I would not return to work and instead become a full-time entrepreneur. I was so determined to work from home because I knew I needed to focus, and working full time wouldn't give me that luxury. I knew I needed money to support my family while I hustled to grow my business, but I didn't know where I was going to get it. Then, I heard about a work-from-home position and submitted my resume. I was immediately called in and hired. I had become an at-home phone operator for Pizza Nova. Yes, you read that right. I went through two years of "Thanks for calling Pizza Nova. How can I help you?" I developed joint pain in my hands due to the amount of work I did.

I never shared that story with anyone, not even my team. I was too embarrassed to admit it. I didn't want anyone to think I was a joke. I mean, what would they think? People saw me in the newspapers and on TV; meanwhile, there I was taking orders from my laptop. Does it sound glamorous? Absolutely not, but sacrifices had to be made. I want you to understand, this is what the initial stage of the start-up phase looks like. It's rough, ugly, and uncomfortable. It's also ***very*** humbling.

My grandmother used to say, "If you want [something] good, your nose has to run." Meaning you have to do the things you don't necessarily like in order to elevate yourself to the next level. For many of us, it's working at a job we despise in order to finance the dream, or perhaps relocating to take advantage of an opportunity. Using your ***Boss Journal***, write down your desires and the things you are willing to give up to achieve them. Once you're done, make your requests known to God, and trust and believe that He will supply all your needs. Keep going! You've got this.

BOSS CHALLENGE #8

Perseverance is the most valuable skill entrepreneurs need in order to survive. While it's not impossible to build perseverance, it does require consistency and determination to grow. I created a step-by-step system to help you develop and sharpen this very important skill. Visit www.tamarhuggins.com/bossedup to download the Perseverance Challenge worksheets.

NOTES

CHAPTER 9

BALANCE

BOSS TRUTH #81

PAUSE

—

"Then God blessed the seventh day and sanctified it, because in it He rested from all His work which God had created and made."
–GENESIS 2:3

Take a moment and just breathe. You're probably on back-to-back phone calls, constantly on your laptop, or running back and forth for meetings. Take time to ***pause***. Remember, the universe and all that is in it was not built in a day. So your business, and all the work you've put into it, will not fall to the ground (or at least it shouldn't) if you take a day off. God, Himself, rested on the seventh day! It wasn't because He needed to, but rather to illustrate to us the importance of rest. If you've built wisely, just as in God's example, then you can take the well-needed rest He's designed for you to have. On each day, He strategically created each system to be able to sustain the next. First, there was light, which started the concept of time. Second, there were the Heavens. Third, He created the earth, seas, grass, trees, and every seed-yielding plant. Then, there was the creation of the sun, moon, and stars on the fourth day. Sea creatures and birds were on the fifth day. Land animals, creatures, and humans were on the sixth day.

The Bible says that He blessed the seventh day and sanctified it, which means that we are not only to rest, but to reverence Him and all that He has done. To sanctify something is to set it apart, so your day of rest should be different from any other day of your week. If God rested and took the time to enjoy his creation, who are we to work ourselves into the ground? You may need to hire staff members to provide support, and adjust your weekly schedule to allow for more personal time. If you haven't built your business to be able to function without you for ***one day***, then it's time to reconsider the structure of your business.

BOSS TRUTH #82

WORK TO LIVE, DON'T LIVE TO WORK

"When you eat the labor of your hands, you shall be happy, and it shall be well with you."
–PSALM 128:2

We are not robots. The work we do should simply be the branches on our "tree of life," and ***not*** the tree itself. You are not what you do. Instead, what you do is an extension of who you are, which makes it more impactful.

It is not God's will for us to work in vain and not enjoy the fruits of our labour. What sense does it make to work just to pay bills and not enjoy a life of fulfillment? Paul speaks of this in 1 Corinthians 9:7. He says, "... who plants a vineyard and does not eat of its fruit? Or who tends a flock and does not drink of the milk of the flock?" Take vacations. Eat at great restaurants. Host celebrations. Do what you love! Who said you can't have fun? All work and no play will cause you to burn out ASAP!

As entrepreneurs, we get up every morning and work until the wee hours of the night. When people are enjoying their REM sleep, we're on our third coffee pushing ourselves to the finish line. I am so guilty of this. I recently accepted that it's OK for me to enjoy my life to the fullest. Since I love what I do, I am always working hard, and it doesn't seem like work to me. It's not until the summer ends that I realize I have no fun stories to talk about! I think to myself, "Where did the time go?!" And I regret not taking the time to enjoy the weather, concerts, and events with those closest to me. If we work hard, we should play hard. Ecclesiastes 8:15 says, "So I commended enjoyment, because a man has nothing better under the sun than to eat, drink, and be merry; for this will remain with him in his labor all the days of his life which God gives him under the sun." What sense does it make to work so hard and not enjoy the dividends? I'm here to tell you that it is OK to enjoy your life. If you haven't been, please start ***immediately***. After all, you only have one life.

As believers with balance, we must also "walk after the Spirit," and not get too caught up in the world's system. Jesus said that "one's life does not consist in the abundance of the things he possesses."[49] This only leads to covetousness. We keep our perspective by understanding that what we do can only be done when our strength and help comes from the Lord. Moreover, realize that God doesn't send His help and strength for there not to be a reward. ***You've come this far, so enjoy what you've made***. God wants us to be successful, and He also wants us to be reapers of what we've sown.

NOTES

BOSS TRUTH #83

WORK FROM ANYWHERE

"For this is the will of God, that by doing good you may put to silence the ignorance of foolish men – as free, yet not using your liberty as a cloak for vice, but as bondservants of God."
–1 PETER 2:15-16

One of the perks of being a boss is that you are in complete control of your schedule. You choose ***when*** you work, ***how*** you work, and ***where*** you work. Actually, most entrepreneurs just need a laptop and internet connection and they can plug in from anywhere in the world. Imagine sitting on the balcony of your hotel suite in Bora Bora just taking in the scenery while responding to client emails or having a virtual meeting with your team. Amazing, isn't it?! Entrepreneurship opens up many doors to flexibility and freedom. You don't have to be confined to an office to get work done, and don't let anyone tell you differently.

The inspiration that awaits you is endless as ***you*** get to choose your own environment and destinations. I love to be surrounded by nature when I work, so I rarely sit inside my office. Most mornings, I will enjoy the natural sunlight in my kitchen or sit on my patio and take in the inspiring beauty of my garden. I like to be at peace when I work, so any environment that provides stillness and visual stimulation is perfect for me – whether it's in my home or in a villa in Costa Rica. Of course, our freedom should never be taken for granted, and we should never use it as a loophole to live unbalanced, scattered lives. When scripture says that we are to live like "bondservants of God," that means He should shine through in all that we do, and our good works should be our vindication in the midst of naysayers. To make it as an entrepreneur, you have to master discipline. Think of your freedom as an opportunity and be careful not to misuse it.

BOSS TRUTH #84

PRIORITIZE FAITH

"But seek first the Kingdom of God and His righteousness, and all these things shall be added to you."
–MATTHEW 6:33

You can always tell when someone is truly yearning for something from the Lord. They faithfully attend church and Bible study, and you always find them at the front of every altar call. Then, after a while, they disappear and we wonder what happened to them! You see what happens when God blesses us with the very thing we want? We get so consumed with it that we prioritize what we've been asking for over serving the Kingdom of God. Sadly, this is a very common cycle. When we put our business over our ministry, church attendance dwindles, prayers cease, and tithing stops. It often takes something dramatic to bring us back into focus with God.

Even though we serve a patient God, don't waste your time going in circles. I admit that in the past, I prioritized ***my*** business over God's business. I became engrossed in my work, and I thought it was alright because I was doing God's will. I didn't pray or study the Word as often as I should have, and I didn't always tithe when I was supposed to. What eventually happened is that my business slowed down, and clients starting paying their invoices months past due. As a result, my cash flow suffered. My heart was being tested, and I realized that even though you can be ***in*** the will of God, it still matters ***how*** you go about it. God reminded me that He comes before my business, and He certainly got my attention!

Now, in the mornings, I prioritize my day by first thanking God for ten things I am grateful for. I put my entire day into His hands and ask for His covering and blessings on my life and my family. I pray every day ***and*** attentively listen for His direction. When I need clarity or guidance, I lock myself away in my prayer closet with worship music, and I just sing and pray. I do this for as long as the Holy Spirit leads me. I've learned that when I make God a priority, everything works seamlessly. God literally has all the time in the world, but we don't. If you're disobedient, He can and will raise up another individual to use for His glory.

Why not prioritize your faith now, so that you don't have to backtrack in your growth? After all, obedience is better than sacrifice.[50] We have to remain just as committed to the things we did ***before*** our blessings came. Don't make the same mistake I did. Learn to put ***God's*** business first and you will see a consistent increase in the finances, opportunities, and growth of ***your*** business.

BOSS TIP

I encourage you to carve out personal time with God. Discover the activities you enjoy doing to get close to Him. Is it singing, dancing, praying, or reading? Whatever it may be, I challenge you to dedicate one hour a day to doing just that and watch breakthroughs happen!

NOTES

BOSS TRUTH #85

PRIORITIZE YOUR FAMILY

"But if anyone does not provide for his own, and especially for those of his household, he has denied the faith and is worse than an unbeliever."
–1 TIMOTHY 5:8

It is so easy to consume ourselves with work and neglect the things and people in our lives that deserve our attention. I am the type of person who cannot rest until the work is done, and I've lived by that philosophy all my life. I knew I was overdoing it when I caught my daughter in my office at my computer one day pretending to be me: "Sorry, I can't talk to you right now; I'm busy!" were the words that came out of her mouth. She was three! It really hurt me to hear her say that. I didn't want to be one of those moms who worked so hard and missed the important moments with her small children. From that day forward, I made a promise to myself to never put my work before spending quality time with my family. Part of the reason I became an entrepreneur was so that I could spend more time with my daughter, but instead the reverse happened. I thank the Holy Spirit for putting me in check at that moment, because it literally saved me from making the very same error I was trying to avoid.

In 1 Timothy 5:8, the Hebrew translation of ***provide*** means to "take thought of, or care for, beforehand."[51] This is essential because money doesn't raise kids, people do. Money also doesn't unify families...people do! What have you truly accomplished if you attain great wealth and success, but your children don't know you, or your marriage falls apart? Take care of the ones you love. In doing so, you'll find your work life to be more rewarding because you can have peace of mind knowing that nothing ***and no one*** is being left behind.

BOSS TRUTH #86

PRIORITIZE YOUR HEALTH

"For you were bought with a price; therefore glorify God in your body and in your spirit, which are God's."
–1 CORINTHIANS 6:20

A business acquaintance once told me to "remember self-care." It sounded so simple at the time, but it stuck with me because deep down I knew she was right. I am a huge advocate for natural medicine, and I've given up on general practitioners because I am convinced that 90% of them only solve problems by pushing drugs we don't need. What we really need to do is learn how to listen to our own bodies. Our body speaks to us in various ways, and the Holy Spirit is with us to reveal all things. However, we are often too disconnected from our inner selves to recognize it. Sometimes we take simple things for granted, such as getting enough rest and detoxing our bodies. Also, emotional and physical stress can cause health issues from eczema to cancer.

We were bought with the price of the blood of Jesus, so let's not waste it. There are – ***at a minimum*** – four things you can put into practice now to improve your health over time:

1. Cook at home more often. The more you plan ahead, the easier meal planning will become. When you purchase ingredients to cook, you are taking charge over what goes into your body instead of passively consuming what major brands and fast food chains call "food."

2. Choose more physical activities. It's understandable that everyone doesn't like to work out, but you can still choose to live an active life. When hanging out with friends, family, or coworkers, intentionally choose activities that get you moving. For example, choose activities such as laser tag or hiking near a waterfall instead of other activities that may have you sitting the majority of the time.

3. Drink water! You will be surprised at the change you feel in your body if you go ***one week*** without sodas and other sugary drinks. Your body is made up of 60% water, and you need to flush your body of toxins if you want to perform at your best.

4. Beat stress. Have a game plan for stress and anxiety, and know what triggers your emotions. Whether it's scriptures you quote, music you listen to, or a relaxing place you retreat to, find your happy place. Also, give yourself a time limit to get over disappointments – don't let one bad day turn into a bad week or a bad month. You are in control!

We all need to push reset and restore our bodies back to their original settings. Your business needs you to operate at full capacity. Just because we ***feel*** good in the moment doesn't mean our body isn't suffering in areas that will eventually manifest in negative ways. Hosea 4:6 says, "My people are destroyed for lack of knowledge..." Listen to what your body is telling you! If you feel there is something you don't understand, begin to research it. My suggestion is to seek advice from a holistic practitioner and learn what your body needs to begin functioning the way God intended it to.

BOSS TIP

I challenge you to schedule one hour a day for yourself. You may choose to read, rest, pray, or exercise. Whatever it is, just do it, and get serious about prioritizing your health. Fit bosses maintain more success! Also, think of the money you can save if you prepare *now* to live a healthy life free from unnecessary hospital bills and prescriptions. There are 24 hours in a day, and you *can* afford to dedicate one to yourself. Strategize how you can live your best life.

NOTES

BOSS TRUTH #87

TRUST ONLY THOSE WHO ARE PROVEN

"Now I urge you, brethren, note those who cause divisions and offenses, contrary to the doctrine which you learned, and avoid them...by smooth words and flattering speech [they] deceive the hearts of the simple."
–ROMANS 16:17-18

I'm not the type of person who allows people to get too close too soon. When it comes to my business, I am extremely careful who I allow in my inner circle. I met a young woman at an event that I was speaking at, and it turned out she had the experience I was looking for in a new educator. She was extremely eager to help, and I must admit, it threw me off a bit. I had to find out whether she was genuine. I am always suspicious when people are overly eager to do anything. So I prayed and asked God to show me who this young woman was. I introduced her to another member of my team, whose insight I trust, and he liked her energy.

As I took the time to get to know her, I learned so much about her character, her spirit, and her work ethic. To my surprise, I learned that she was a devout Christian like me and wasn't afraid to show it. In the beginning, I was cautious; however, I remembered asking God to enlarge my team and He was answering my prayers! I now have another valuable member on my team who I trust to do exactly what they say they will do. When you have people on your team who you can trust, it makes balancing other areas of your business much easier to do.

Let me keep it real with you, many of the people who don't want to see you succeed exist in your social media groups, inner circles, and even your family. The Lord wants you to know that many enemies will seek to infiltrate your camp and sabotage your work, but more are for you than against you.[36] I want you to be open to adding new people to your team, but take the time to get to know the individual you want to hire as they will become part of your extended family. Furthermore, it's OK to share your dreams and ambitions with others, but be mindful as ***there's a time to keep silent, and a time to speak***.[37]

BOSS TRUTH #88

MANAGE YOUR MONEY WELL

"There is desirable treasure,
And oil in the dwelling of the wise,
But a foolish man squanders it."
–PROVERBS 21:20

One of the things I wish I knew when I became an entrepreneur was how important my personal finances were to my business. It's a natural inclination to pour all your money into your company, but if you don't have a backup plan, you're screwed – point, blank, period. Take it from me, the "starving artist" lifestyle is not cute and should be avoided at all costs. When I started, I had office rent to pay, lawyer fees, you name it! I was a young, black female and didn't want to be stereotyped, so I put the finances of my business ahead of my own and ended up in debt that eventually went to collections. I tried everything to avoid consolidation, but it was the only way I would get out of my situation alive.

Let me tell you, pride is a dangerous thing! It will have you "keeping up appearances" and making sacrifices that you'll regret later. It's a silent struggle that all entrepreneurs go through. I was so concerned about building my reputation that my credit suffered for it, and it took two years to rebuild it again. Reality hit me when I tried to officially open a business bank account and obtain a business credit card. I was declined because the bank looked at my personal credit history in lieu of my business (because it had none). It was devastating but I knew I would have to make wiser decisions in future.

I advise you to seek guidance in managing your personal finances, ***and stick to the plan***. You must learn the importance of being a good steward over the money God has entrusted you with. I understand that finances are private, and you may not always feel comfortable sharing them, so choose to work with someone you feel you can trust. I always invest 30% of my income in areas where I can see a decent return, such as real estate and stocks. Do what is comfortable for you, and what makes sense for your situation. Handle your money in such a manner that God will be pleased. After all, that's what makes the treasure of the wise desirable – the fact that it is obtained through exemplary means. Those with wisdom plan well and consider the long-term effects of their spending.

BOSS TRUTH #89

MAKE TIME TO SUPPORT OTHERS

"Behold, how good
and how pleasant it is for brethren
to dwell together in unity."
–PSALM 133:1

Often, we get so busy in our own world that we fail to see the needs of others. We never hesitate to ask our network of friends and close business associates to support and promote everything we are doing, but how much do ***you*** support ***them***? How many events have you attended in support of others? How many times have you asked, ***"What can I do to help?"*** The principle of sisterhood is deeply rooted in the Word of God, and even many of the sermons of Jesus. This is not the only reason you should be willing to support what others are doing, but in chapter 2 you learned that collaborations and affiliations can take your business to the next level. Be a visible face or helping hand in ways that you would want if you were in their position. We have to see them as fellow runners on this entrepreneurial track.

One of the keys to maintaining successful business relationships is genuine communication. In your circle or community of business owners, begin to listen more intently to the needs and experiences of others. It is important to nurture those relationships and approach every situation with a ***"How can I help you?"*** mentality. Let's destroy the stereotype that women are too selfish to support others. Empowered women empower women!

BOSS TRUTH #90

BE FULLY INVESTED IN ALL YOU DO

"I can do all things through Christ who strengthens me."
–PHILIPPIANS 4:13

When Apostle Paul made this statement in Philippians 4:13, what he was saying is, "I can ***endure and accomplish*** all things through Christ, who strengthens me." He was prosperous ***and*** destitute at the same time. He was celebrated and he was persecuted. The foundation on which he stood was the strength of Christ, and his outpour was unwavering because he had learned the power of consistency through contentment. What he did for the Kingdom never depended on what he had or how many obstacles he was facing. This should be our confession as well – "no matter what my life looks like, I will ***consistently*** produce!"

Having balance in your life doesn't mean you give 50/50; it means you give 100/100. If Paul didn't give his all, we wouldn't have the majority of the New Testament. Many churches would not have been formed and its leaders never developed. Consider what (or who) is dependent on you giving your all, because you can't afford to be unbalanced. You may ask whether it's possible to give 100% to both your personal life and business, and the answer is yes. We can do all things through Christ, for He is the source of our strength! Doing things on our own strength is tiring, and it is not proper stewardship as the ambassadors we are called to be. If you face a challenging situation, trust that He has a plan to optimize your life. If you want it, you can achieve it, and don't settle for anything less. Commit to every aspect of your life with passion. Be fully invested in all you do.

BOSS CHALLENGE #9

Visit www.tamarhuggins.com/bossedup to download the 30-day Personal and Business Detox Challenge. Identify areas of your life that could use a good detox. This can be a social media detox, a physical detox, or even a detox from certain people or habits. Your goal is to develop healthy habits and remove inhibiting toxicity from your life.

NOTES

CHAPTER 10

VICTORIOUS

BOSS TRUTH #91

YOU DIDN'T COME THIS FAR ONLY TO COME THIS FAR

"For surely there is a hereafter [future], And your hope will not be cut off."
–PROVERBS 23:18

You may feel like you've planted seeds in a dry season, and you may be asking the Lord, ***"Where is my harvest?"*** You've prayed for months (maybe even a few years), and you may feel like the Lord hasn't heard you, but He has! Don't abort your hope because ***there is*** victory coming for you. He is not going to leave you in your current situation. He both delivers ***and*** He prospers those who are rooted in Him. He knows the desires of your heart before you even know them. You must petition the rain to come. The "rain" is connected to your blessings, and you have to nurture the seeds you've already planted. Many people are asking for more and greater, but they haven't expended themselves at their current level. Just be sure you've maxed out your present potential first before becoming frustrated with God. He doesn't send rain to the harvest until He knows it's the right time.

Think about a potted plant. If it's growing and flourishing in its current pot, you're not going to replant it to a bigger pot until its roots have reached a certain level of maturity. If you do so prematurely, you run the risk of stressing the plant, even to the point of killing it. This is exactly how God views us. You fit in one of two categories: either (1) you've truly outgrown your "pot" and are in dire need of God to send His rain and expansion for you to move forward, ***or*** (2) you've still got "leaves and roots" to fill out before you can handle the capacity of something bigger. Either way, don't be afraid to remind the Lord of your faithfulness and commitment, but know where you are and ***how*** you need Him to move. Believe in your heart and in the Spirit that the blessings you so desperately need are in fact on their way. Declare it now, and be open to receive all that the Lord has for you!

BOSS TRUTH #92

EVERY DIFFERENT LEVEL DEMANDS A DIFFERENT YOU

"...walk worthy of the calling with which you were called."
–EPHESIANS 4:1

When you're doing God's work, the enemy will come against you hard. If he doesn't, then you are not a threat to him. You may get knocked down one hundred times and feel like you're down for the last count, but I'm here to tell you that if you can look up, you can get up! What the devil means for evil, God will turn around for your good. Your future self is dependent on the preparations you make now to defeat stronger enemies and stronger opposition. Even if this doesn't seem relevant right now, you have to constantly remain in a place of growing and maturing so that victory can flow freely in your life and business.

Part of Ephesians 4:14-15 says, "...we should no longer be children tossed to and fro...but...may grow up in all things into Him who is the head – Christ." We are called to grow up in ***all*** things, and that growth looks different at different levels. The promises and prophecies you received from God are contingent upon ***you*** being able to handle them effectively, without compromise. Defeat is not in your nature, and as your victory comes, it will require you to adapt to a new level of Christ-likeness that you have yet to experience. Trust your calling, and walk worthy of it! Trust Him to be your anchor and foundation, because it's not over until God says it's done! What seems impossible is God's chance to work a miracle...even if that miracle is within you! I urge you to trust Him. Hold your head up and know you're going to win.

BOSS TRUTH #93

YOU ARE THE HEAD, NOT THE TAIL

"And the Lord will make you the head and not the tail; you shall be above only, and not be beneath, if you heed the commandments of the Lord your God, which I commanded you today, and are careful to observe them."
–DEUTERONOMY 28:13

I know the God I serve; He is great and mighty. You and I are reflections of His image, and He sets us above our enemies! What He requires is our obedience and faithfulness. God says that we are above only and ***not beneath***, we are lenders and not borrowers, and His Word cannot come back to Him void. So we must believe we are all that He says we are and walk in boldness and confidence knowing that our steps are ordered and protected by the Lord. With certain levels of success, it can be easy for guilt or fear to creep in, but don't allow it.

One of the enemy's attempts is to make you feel guilty for excelling as far as you have, but you don't have to apologize for being great! Many times, I experienced others trying to downplay my success because it exposed their weaknesses. All I try to do is live my life according to the Word and be ***exactly*** who God said I am: the ***head*** and not the tail. Don't allow the size of your success to diminish how you embrace and celebrate it. If you were born for it, then you can flourish in it!

BOSS TRUTH #94

YOU HAVE POWER OVER THE ENEMY

"Behold, I give you the authority to trample on serpents and scorpions, and over all the power of the enemy, and nothing shall by any means harm you."
–LUKE 10:19

Don't be afraid of the arrows that come from the enemy, because God has already given us the authority to defeat him. We must fight in the Spirit because in the flesh, we will never win. The Word of God tells us that no weapon formed against us will prosper,[52] but it never said we wouldn't have to fight. The weapons formed against you are not carnal but spiritual, and there are many. Go ahead and get physical fights out of your mind because to achieve the type of victory God wants you to have, you must learn to temper yourself. ***And*** along with this, you must maintain the stance of Satan being crushed under your feet.[53]

You must engage in spiritual battle because we are fighting spiritual forces that simply use physical circumstances (or people) to come against us. That is why 2 Corinthians 10:3-4 says, "For though we walk in the flesh we do not war according to the flesh. For the weapons of our warfare are not carnal but mighty in God…" The ***"in God"*** part is so vital to understand because – in your own ability – ***you*** can do nothing; it is the blood of Jesus that gives us access to Heavenly power and ultimate victory. This is why God calls us to put on the entire armour of God, and – ***with it*** – no weapon formed against us shall prosper! Ephesians 6:13-17 says we are to have the belt of truth, the breastplate of righteousness, our feet prepared with the gospel of peace, the shield of faith, the helmet of salvation, and the sword that is the Word of God. If you put all these together, you have the full armour of God, which prepares you for the battlefield.

Warfare can be some of the toughest seasons in our lives and can include encounters and experiences that others wouldn't believe, but stand strong – you've already been given the essentials to make it through. Speak words of victory over yourself. The power of life and death are in the power of your own tongue. Pressures are all around, ***but God is present help***. The enemy creates walls, but God causes giants to fall. Believe and receive it. You ***have*** triumphed over your enemies.

BOSS TRUTH #95

EXPECT THE SUPERNATURAL

"Immediately he arose, took up the bed, and went out in the presence of them all, so that all were amazed and glorified by God, saying, 'We never saw anything like this!'"
—MARK 2:12

God is about to blow your mind. Let expectation fill your heart as you prepare for the glory of God to take over. You were destined to be a glory carrier – the avenue through which God shows His supernatural power! The Word of God says that "the earth is full of His glory"[54] and we are part of that glory as His creation...we just need to have the faith to yield to it. Just like it was faith that unlocked the supernatural with the paraplegic in Mark 2:5, we are supposed to believe God in that same magnitude.

What are you believing God for? Is it to finally live your dream of doing what you love? Or perhaps it's generating a six-figure income this year. When you truly believe God for the supernatural, it doesn't matter who around you is not in agreement. The Word says, "The eyes of the Lord run to and fro throughout the whole earth, to show Himself strong on behalf of those whose heart is loyal to Him."[55] So keep your heart loyal and don't be found in a place of unbelief when He is desiring to be strong in you and for you. To expect the supernatural is also to expect misunderstandings from those around you. Some may not understand your passion, and they may not be able to tread the depths of where you're going. It can feel lonely at times, but that's OK! In the Bible, before God did supernatural work in the earth realm, He called ***out*** those whose ears were inclined to Him. After drawing them close and imparting His vision into their hearts, He would send them back out among people to spread His glory. Just remember, we serve ***Jehovah-Jireh***, the God who provides, and He will sustain you.

Before the miracle in Mark 2:12, those that were with the paraplegic bombarded the room Jesus was in; they even went through the roof and ***made space where there was none*** so that Jesus could perform miracles. Are you bombarding the feet of Jesus? Are you positioning yourself and your business for the supernatural power of God to flow? Think on these things because His glory has a purpose. Just like the crowd's response was "We never saw anything like this," He is desiring to shock the world with what He can do through you!

So ***choose*** to embrace the supernatural! Expect it! Also, no matter how high you go, never compare your business model to others. Compare it to Heaven's particular design for you, because even if you surpass what others in your industry are doing, you're ***still*** not fulfilling your true potential and capacity in God until what you're producing in the earth matches His will. The trademark of the believer is to have God's supernatural power flowing through everything we do. Jesus set a standard for us to show us what our "normal" should look like, and we should never deviate from that. So ***ask*** God to multiply. ***Ask*** Him to heal and calm the storm. Ask Him to supernaturally grow and produce what has never been seen before! Prepare to be amazed.

NOTES

BOSS TRUTH #96

PUT YOUR CROWN ON BEFORE YOU LEAVE THE HOUSE

"You shall also be a crown of glory in the hand of the Lord, And a royal diadem in the hand of your God."
–ISAIAH 62:3

Just as we are crowns in the hands of God, our light will shine brightly wherever we go. The word ***diadem*** from the scripture means: a crown that is worn especially by a king or queen as a symbol of royalty.[56] We are spiritual jewels in the earth, and our attitudes and demeanors should be reflective as such. Don't allow the "temperature" of the world to determine how or who you are. Set the atmosphere wherever you go. Smile even if everyone else is frowning. Be kind when others are mean. Live and laugh in the face of adversity!

Putting your crown on is a mindset. When you dress yourself in the morning, dress your mind for the success and victory of the day. Be prepared to walk tall and confident because you are royal heirs, and your crown will shine each day. We are meant to be a light in the earth, and the light of God will beam through us wherever we go. People should see a difference when they work with us, when they speak with us, and when they are in our presence because we are carrying ourselves as crowns of glory. We no longer represent ourselves when we do business, but we represent the One who sent us.

Isaiah 62:3 is referring to God's view of Jerusalem – ***His*** holy city and the people His heart beats for. This relates to us because now **we** (as Christians) are the people His heart beats for as well. Romans 8:15-17 says we have *"received the spirit of adoption by whom we cry out 'Abba, Father.' The Spirit Himself bears witness with our spirit that we are children of God, and if children, then heirs - heirs of God and joint heirs with Christ, if indeed we suffer with Him that we may also be glorified together."* This is an important scripture because it makes all the difference in how we view our lives. It lets us know that our royalty in God is contingent, because to be joint heirs with Christ, there is also suffering with Him. But praise God there are rewards in the end!

Therefore, just because you've suffered doesn't mean you have to ***look like it***. Don't miscarry or misrepresent the light and the glory that God has given you. We are princes and princesses in the eyes of our God and He has given us keys to the Kingdom of Heaven.[57] Unlock it in your business! Establish His rulership and be a walking symbol of victory for all to see.

NOTES

BOSS TRUTH #97

IT'S NEVER TOO LATE TO START!

"For Sarah conceived and bore Abraham a son in his old age, at the set time of which God had spoken to him."
–GENESIS 21:2

You could be in your twenties ***or*** your forties at the beginning of your new career. It doesn't matter who you are or how old you are – the time to start is now. Seasons come and go, and opportunities don't last forever. If you haven't begun your journey toward entrepreneurship yet, assess all the time you've spent thinking about it, being too nervous, or feeling too inadequate for it. Hopefully, at this point in the book, you've been encouraged and uplifted concerning your ability to make it as your own boss. So, what's holding you back?

If it's finances, pray about it, find the resources you need, and get to work. If there's a degree you need, go to school and get it. If it's leaders you need, search for them. Begin to pursue the promises God has made concerning your life. The Word of God says that both Abraham ***and*** Sarah laughed at the thought of bearing a child in their old age, but God's promise came true. What are some things God has said to ***you*** that you simply laughed at? If He said it will happen, He's going to make it happen. It takes the fullness of God's Spirit operating in you to accomplish His plans.

The difference between Sarah and us is that ***God*** made the decision to approach her in her old age to illustrate that supernatural things can happen at any point of our lives – but only if we believe. While I was writing this book, I decided that I wanted to reach readers all over the world. It's not common for a new or self-published author to receive international distribution for their first book, but I believed that God would enlarge my territory. I reached out to the number one book distributor in the U.S., and within four days I received an e-mail from their president stating that my book (the one you're reading now) was approved for global distribution. This was a huge accomplishment for me being a first-time author. I set high expectations, and I met them, because I believed God's word.

You have a choice right now to get started on things that are overdue. Tomorrow, you'll wish you started today. It will all line up, and things will fall into place. It's never too late to start.

BOSS TRUTH #98

DON'T ALLOW PEOPLE TO MISPRONOUNCE YOUR NAME

"But now, O Lord, You are our Father; We are the clay, and You our potter; And all we are the work of Your hand."
–ISAIAH 64:8

The names we have been given are very important! It doesn't matter if you were teased about it as a child or if you just don't like it. Don't allow anyone to mispronounce your name! It is about respect. This is especially true for those of us with uncommon names and even uncommon spellings. Your name is worth the effort. Also realize that the name God gave you is a part of who you are. Personally, I didn't like my name as a child because it wasn't common. I would cringe every time a new teacher took our class attendance, because they always pronounced my name wrong. I got to the point where I felt it necessary to correct anyone who mispronounced my name. When misunderstandings happen, pause and take the time to politely correct people. Let it be known what ***you*** want to be called.

Do not allow people to call you by childish, undermining, or derogatory nicknames. Such names can carry a stigma that undermines your identity and the level of excellence you are more than able to produce. This is not to say that all nicknames are bad. We just have to think ahead and calculate the image we want to present to those around us. Our words have no sense of humour. Whatever we speak becomes reality. We are the work of God's hands, just like the clay is to the potter, and I believe that He desires for us to value ourselves just as much as He does. God wants us to be confident in who He has called us to be.

BOSS TRUTH #99

YOU ARE VALIDATED

"For do I now persuade men, or God? Or do I seek to please God? For if I still pleased men, I would not be a bondservant of Christ."

—GALATIANS 1:10

Validation...it's an innate feeling of belonging that we want to experience from a very young age. From childhood, it's so important for us to know that we are doing the right thing or that our parents are pleased. As children, we are taught to ask for permission for the smallest of things, and we're even groomed to look up to those around us (even if the influences weren't always positive). That same respect and reverence we gave our parents should be given to God. Now, we are to look to Him as being the one who is pleased with us and gives us permission to do certain things.

Unfortunately, many adults are still seeking the approval of others for the simplest of things. I'm going to tell you something you absolutely need to know: ***God validated you the day you were born.*** Write that down and etch it in your brain, because I need you to understand it. Why are you putting yourself through the stress of seeking validation from those whose opinions, quite frankly, don't matter? I remember in 2009 when I began my entrepreneurial journey, some people didn't support me. Even family members couldn't understand what I was doing, or why it was so important to work for myself instead of someone else. They couldn't support the idea of entrepreneurship because they didn't understand how I saw it and what I was aiming for. For them, success meant going to work in a suit with a briefcase in hand. So when I didn't meet their expectations, they assumed I wasn't doing anything important.

It was hurtful, not getting the validation I felt I needed at the time, but I knew I was answering a call that God had placed on my life from birth. I was destined to shape the world through entrepreneurship, and I knew I had God's approval to do so. Without faith, we cannot please God. We cannot call ourselves followers of Christ if we are still trying to please others. Who are you seeking approval from to start your business? Could it be your spouse, family, or friends? You only need to seek approval from God – who is your provider and Lord over your life.

BOSS TRUTH #100

YOU ARE THE WINNER

"Many daughters have done well, but you excel them all."
–PROVERBS 31:29

On October 10, 2012, I lost my aunt to cancer. She was a mother to me, and I was devastated. Two days before she passed, she called me to her bedside, peered into my eyes, and said her last words to me: "You are the winner. You are the winner. You ARE the winner!" I couldn't understand why she was saying it, especially as she was dying. I soon came to realize that her words had a purpose, and it was a reminder of the victorious power that God placed within me. Her four-word phrase has gotten me through many tough times and situations when I was ready to quit.

I feel so humbled and honored to receive the assignment that I have. I do not take it lightly! Sometimes I look back at my life and think "Man, I never thought I'd be here!" I always knew I was destined for greatness, but I never understood how deep it would go. Still, "To whom much is given, much is required," so I'm passing this encouragement on to you: **YOU** are the winner! There is nothing you will face that you can't conquer. God isn't finished with you yet. You are His vessel, and He has called me to help you. Greatness lives within you. Possibility lives within you. God is calling you. Will you answer? Extraordinary potential awaits. Believe that you are ready.

BOSS CHALLENGE #10

Write a letter to your future self and list ten radical things you will do to make your future memoirs worth reading. In the letter, tell yourself what you plan to leave behind with your legacy. How will your legacy live on? How are you laying the foundation now to create massive impact in the future? Be sure to date the letter and reflect on it every year. I want you to know that it is OK if your goals shift, so long as you remain in the will of God for your life.

NOTES

ENDNOTES

1. Bullinger, Ethelbert. *A Critical Lexicon and Concordance to the English and Greek New Testament. Zondervan, 1975.*

2. Strong, James. *Strong's Exhaustive Concordance of the Bible. Zondervan, 1890. http://Biblehub.com/greek/1382.htm*

3. Matthew 16:21-23

4. Matthew 26:51-54, John 18:10-11

5. Matthew 17:4-5

6. John 21:15-17

7. Acts 2:14-47, Acts 3:4-9

8. Microsoft. *Attention Spans Research Report. Canada, 2015.*

9. A live video streaming/broadcasting app from *Twitter.*

10. John 14:12

11. Romans 12:11

12. 1 Samuel 17:48-51

13. Nehemiah 2:8

14. Sorge, Bob. *Secrets of the Secret Place, 196*

15. Galatians 3:29

16. Luke 6:38

17. Deuteronomy 8:18

18. Job 36:11

19. Daniel 3

20. Luke 2:52

21. Matthew 5:13-16

22. 1 Corinthians 4:20

23. Daniel 5:20

24. Titus 2:7

25. James 3:17

26. Isaiah 49:15b-16

27. Galatians 3:26

28. John 15:1-8

29. 2 Corinthians 5:17

30. Genesis 17:5

31. Genesis 17:15

32. Genesis 32:28

33. John 1:42

34. Deuteronomy 34:9

35. Psalm 75:6-7

36. 2 Kings 6:16

37. Ecclesiastes 3:7b

38. 1 Samuel 15:11

39. Genesis 12

40. Genesis 15:5

41. Genesis 5:17

42. Proverbs 6:6-8

43. Proverbs 18:9

44. 2 Timothy 2:6

45. Romans 8:28

46. Isaiah 53:4

47. Romans 8:38-39

48. Hebrews 13:16

49. Luke 12:15

50. 1 Samuel 15:22

51. Strong, James. *Strong's Exhaustive Concordance of the Bible. Zondervan, 1890. http://www.godrules.net/library/strongs2b/gre4306.htm*

52. Isaiah 54:17

53. Romans 16:20

54. Isaiah 6:3

55. 2 Chronicles 16:9

56. Merriam-Webster's Collegiate Dictionary. *11th ed., s.v. "diadem." Also available at http://www.merriam-webster.com/.*

57. Matthew 16:19